GUIDE TO FISHING

VOLUME 1

IN ASSOCIATION WITH

First published in 2016 by Korda Developments Ltd.
PO Box 6313, Basildon, Essex, SS14 0HW.

www.korda.co.uk

ISBN: 978-0-9567875-2-1

Illustrations by John Hannent at www.aitch2.co.uk

Welcome to The Big Fish Off Guide to Fishing Volume 1!

We are extremely proud of the work we have done as a team to bring this show to your screens. Apart from making entertaining TV, our mission was always to inspire more anglers to take up our wonderful sport. However, we also wanted to raise awareness of the spectacular array of different species and show just how easy they can be to catch, if you choose the right venue and the correct methods.

At the start of our fishing lives we focused on a number of smaller species, before slowly working our way up the size spectrum, finally concentrating on the elusive monster! One element we've never lost sight of is just how much we learned as we progressed through, catching different species. It made us the rounded anglers we are today, and more appreciative of every species we catch. This book gives us the chance to give you a detailed look at the tactics and techniques that we can't squeeze into the TV shows!

If The Big Fish Off was to represent a major angling ethos, it's to get out there, learn to catch different species, respect the environment you're in and, most of all, enjoy it!

Big love and thanks for your continued support...

Ali Hamidi & Dean Macey

CONTENTS

THE BIG FISH OFF GUIDE TO FISHING

CHAPTER 1 GETTING STARTED WITH YOUR OWN BIG FISH OFF ADVENTURE

If you've been enjoying the antics of the Big Fish Off crew and want to take up fishing, improve your skills or just learn more, the good news is that we're here to help! This chapter will help you catch your first fish and develop the basic skills you need to be a great angler and catch lots of different species, as well as enjoying being outdoors and learning about the fascinating variety of species and the environments they live in.

It's traditional to kiss your first fish before returning it carefully to the water! AK didn't want to get too close, though.

The easiest way to get started, as Sally Gunnell and Anna Kelle found during their first session on the bank with Dean and Ali, is to use something called a whip (or sometimes a pole) – a tapered carbon or fibreglass pole with line, a float, weights and a hook tied to the end. It's the 21st century version of the cane, string and bent pin! A pole is similar but it has a short length of elastic inside the tip that cushions the lunges from larger fish with a small connector to fix the line to.

A whip or pole is easy to use because simply there isn't much that can go wrong.

There's not much line to tangle and you can simply swing out the rig (the collective name for the line, float, weights and hook), strike when the float goes down and then swing the fish in to unhook. It's a great way to learn basic angling skills before you progress onto using a more complicated rod and reel.

Dean with a beautiful rudd caught by Sally Gunnell - maybe this colourful species will be your first fish?

DID YOU KNOW?

Fishing with a rod and line, known as angling due to the use of an 'angled' hook, was first documented in Japan nearly 11,000 years ago but came to Europe with the Norman conquests in around 1066. By the 1600s, angling had become a popular pastime in England. Izaak Walton published a famous book called The Compleat Angler in 1653, which details many of the modern angling techniques still used today. Except, perhaps, the use of frogs as bait!

Success! AK steers a rudd towards the bank on her first session using an elasticated pole.

A pole or whip is easy to transport as it collapses down into one section, like a Russian doll. The pole at the bottom can extend to more than 10m!

BUYING TACKLE

In order to go fishing, you need some fishing tackle! There are lots of well-stocked fishing tackle shops around the country and these are great places to go to buy your first pole and the items you need to start fishing. The list below covers everything you need to get started.

SHOPPING LIST

- 2-4m Team Daiwa Speed Whip
- Ready-made pole rigs tied to match the length of the whip (e.g. so a 3m whip requires a 3m-long rig)
- Some ready-tied barbless hooks, size 18. The smaller the number, the bigger the hook! Size 20 is tiny - size 1 is huge...
- Some spare weights, called split shot, in case you lose any. A small tub with a variety of sizes is ideal.
- Disgorger to aid unhooking
- Landing net to safely land any larger fish you may hook
- Seat to ensure you're comfortable
- Small landing net and handle
- Rod rest
- Bait tub to hold your bait
- Maggots (1/2 a pint will be fine for a couple of hours – red and white is a good bet)
- A bag to store your tackle in

Team Dean made a great choice of swim at Churchgate, with a comfortable area to fish from, lots of features nearby and fish topping in front of them.

Once you have these items, it's time to plan your session. Just like The Big Fish Off, it's a good idea to start at a venue which is easy to fish and contains a few different species. Lots of fisheries will have a beginner lake designed for people starting fishing and this is a great option – Dean and Ali took Sally Gunnell and Anna Kelle to one such venue, Churchgate Lakes in Essex. It is well stocked with smaller species, has good access and is comfortable and safe. A ticket to fish usually costs £5-10 with cheaper tickets available for juniors and OAPs.

Once you arrive at the venue and you've worked out which lake to fish (the fishery staff will be happy to help), the next task is to find a good 'peg' to set up in. A peg, also known as a swim, is the name for the area you're going to fish. Often, each peg will have a number for when they're used in competitions, known as matches. It's a great idea to ask the fishery owner, official or bailiff (the person who runs the lake and sells the tickets enabling you to fish there) where the best pegs are – they'll know the water well and will be able to direct you towards an area that holds a few fish.

Failing that, you can use your most useful items of tackle to find out where to fish – your eyes!

By looking for signs of fish you will know where to begin your session. You may see them swimming just below the surface in warmer weather, breaking the surface ('dimpling') as they feed, producing bubbles or stirring up the bottom as they search for food, nudging features such as lily pads and reeds as they swim by or maybe you'll see another angler catching in a particular area. Take into account all these things to make a guess at the best spot to try first.

Weed beds, lily pads, reeds and overhanging trees or bushes are all ideal areas to fish near. How many features can you spot in this photo?

At the start of the lad's session with Anna Kelle and Sally, Dean and Ali made sure that their chosen peg had signs of fish – small species like rudd and roach swim in shoals and it's easy to find signs of them if you take a few minutes to walk around the lake, taking care to be quiet (tread gently and don't raise your voice) and avoiding silhouetting yourself against the skyline. Fish can be wary and it's a good idea not to give them any clue that you're there!

DID YOU KNOW?

On bright days the sun's rays bounce off the surface of the water making it difficult to see. A pair of polarising sunglasses and a peaked hat cut down this glare and allow you to see much more below the surface, helping you find some great fishing spots and see your float!

Fishing close to these features is a good idea - but not too close so the fish can take your rig into the snaggy roots and stems.

If you can't see any signs of fish, don't despair – just like people, fish will have their homes where they like to hang out. Find these areas and you'll be certain of a few bites! Overhanging trees, reed beds, lily pads and deeper areas all provide sanctuary for fish and these are good places to start fishing near to. If you're unsure or can't find any signs of your quarry, it's a great idea to ask the fishery staff or a fellow angler where they'd suggest.

Once you've decided on your peg, it's time to get your tackle set up. The type of chair you might take camping is a good, inexpensive option and being comfortable and able to fish effectively is important. Position your chair so you're comfortable and near to the water, a foot or two back from the bank with your landing net at hand for larger fish (2oz or more) and bait tub.

Ready-tied rigs are reliable option for anyone starting out pole or whip fishing - even experts use them!

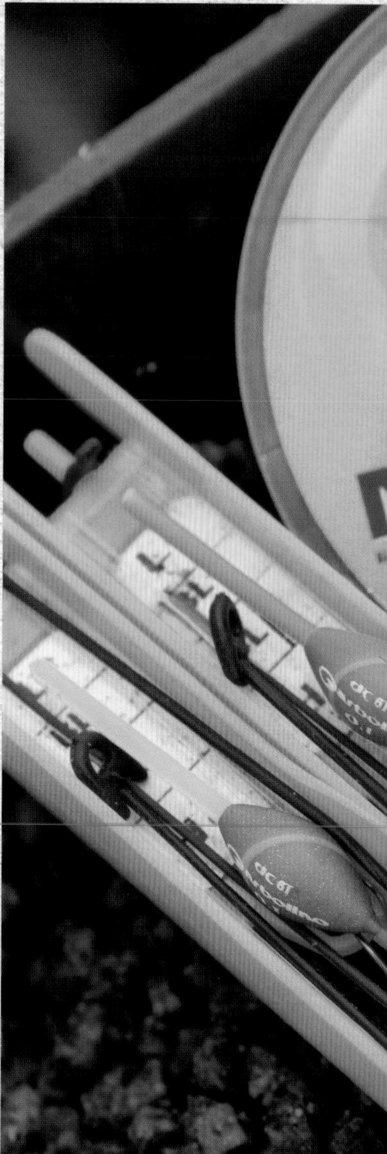

Next, it's time to get your whip (or pole) set up. Extend the whip to its full length – ideally for a beginner this should be between 2 and 4m (depending on age and size) and then attach a rig to the end of the pole using a blood or grinner knot. You might have to get someone to help you tie this or a good idea is to learn at home using one of the many online tutorials – search Google for the name of the knot you wish to tie and lots of short videos will be available to assist. This knot is important as it connects the rig to your pole, so make sure it's strong enough!

Buying ready-tied rigs is also a good idea for the beginner. They're inexpensive and tied by experts!

Whilst Ali and Dean have years of experience and know the correct knots and tackle to use, it's easier to ask an expert in a tackle shop for their recommendations on what rig will be suitable. You can then just tie the rig to the pole, ensuring the length of the rig is the same as that of the pole or whip you're using so you swing the rig to your hand when you want to rebait or unhook a fish.

A small float taking between 1 and 2g is a good all-round choice and a pole float – one that has a delicate stem for stability and a bright tip to show bites – is the ideal model to try first. The small weights, known as 'split shot' or just 'shot', grip onto the line and sink the hook bait to the desired depth, as well as settling the float down to the bright tip so when a fish bites, it goes under and indicates a bite.

You can get several sizes of shot to suit different sizes of float so it's worth having a dispenser containing different sizes in-case you lose a shot or two off the rig. It's important to make sure the bright bit of the float is just visible.

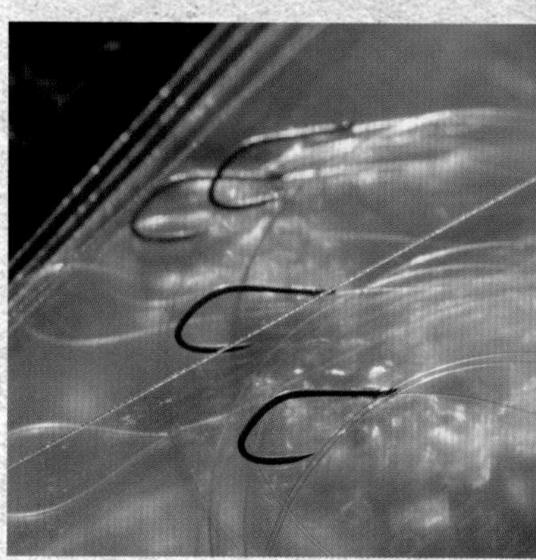

Hooks should be small and barbless – size 18 is a good starting point for single or double maggot hook baits.

Pre-tied hooks come attached to line with a small loop in the end, making them easy to attach to your rig, should the hook become blunt or the rig tangled.

You can buy packets of ready-tied hooks along with a couple of spare pole rigs, allowing you to change the hook length (the bit of line with the hook on – it's often made of lower breaking strain line than the rest of the rig so, should it become stuck on a snag, you will only lose the hook) easily if it becomes tangled or damaged.

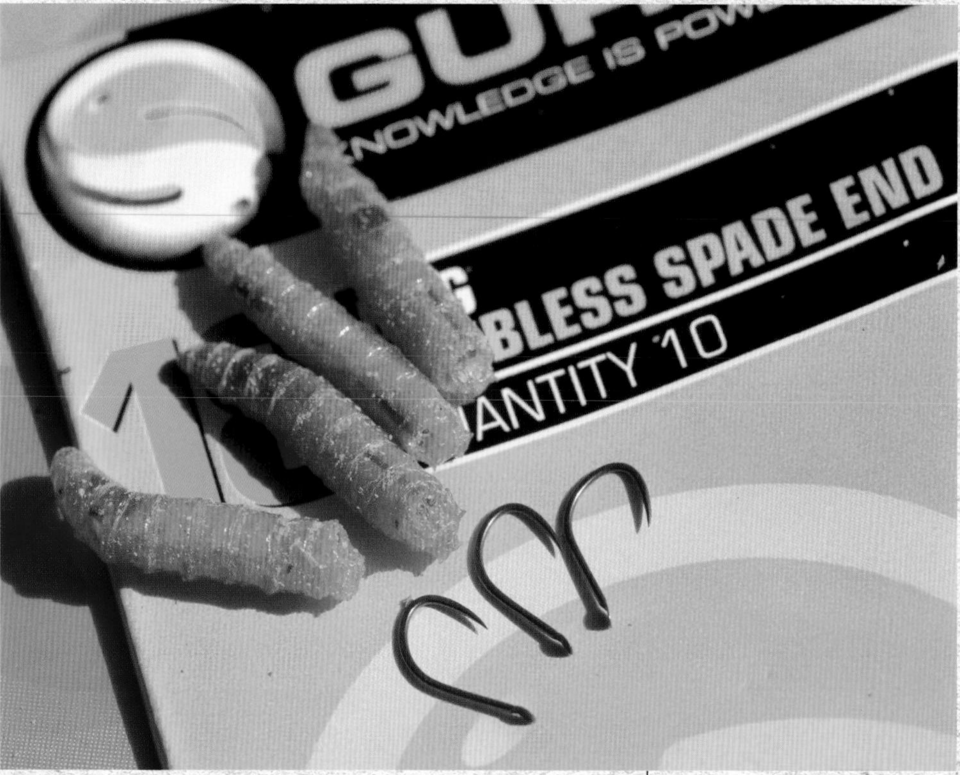

The humble maggot and a small barbless hook is a great combination for lots of different species.

For smaller species, it's best to position the float so they bait is presented midwater – somewhere between the surface and bottom. This is the area most frequently inhabited by species such as roach, perch and rudd and it ensures you won't get caught on weed or snags on the bottom.

Now you've got your whip (or pole) set up with the float set at half the estimated depth of the water in front of you, it's time start fishing! You need to bait your hook first, and a single maggot is a good choice for the size of hook and species you hope to catch. Red or white maggots are good colours to start with, so grab whichever one you fancy between finger and thumb, gently squeezing it so a small tab pops up at the blunt 'head' end of the grub (identified by two dots that look like eyes). This little tab is the best place to hook a maggot, and to do so, gently ease the point of the hook through the tab and down the bend of the hook so it hangs below, wriggling enticingly. If the maggot bursts, start again.

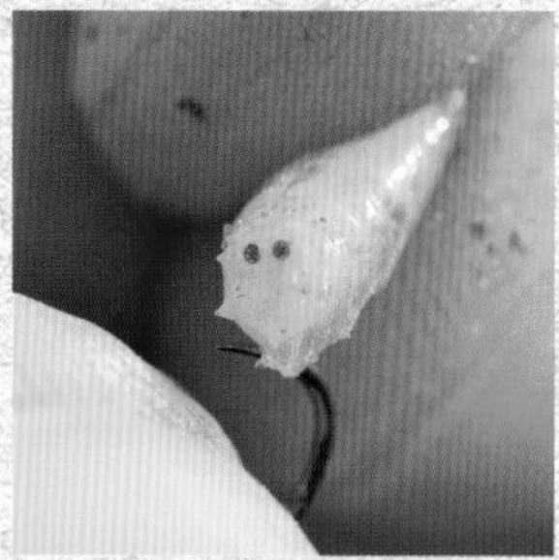

To hook a maggot, squeeze it between your thumb and forefinger. A little tab will pop out, which you can hook.

Mick Wilkinson shallow stemmed float that takes five No.10 shot
4lb N-Gauge main line
Five No.10 shot, evenly strung out.
3lb N-Gauge tied to a size 18 LWG
SHALLOW POLE RIG

Marsh Farm Fishery in Surrey is a fantastic club-run complex.

With this type of equipment, a whip, you don't cast as you might do with a rod and reel – instead, you simply swing the rig out, starting in an upright position and using an 'underarm' swinging action to propel the rig out to where the fish are. Once the float lands, the weights will sink and the float will sit upright and sink down so just the brightly coloured tip is showing. You're now fishing!

When the float lands, it's important to feed some maggots to entice fish into the area and get them feeding.

A small handful of 10-20 maggots at a time is sufficient. Make sure you repeat this at regular intervals; every five minutes is a good starting point.

Hopefully you'll get a bite quickly, if fish are in the swim you've chosen. This will be indicated by the float moving and disappearing under the water. When this happens, you need to strike. A strike is when you lift the pole up to hook the fish, this takes some practice to get right – too gently and you won't hook the fish and it'll get away, or too hard and the fish will be pulled out of the water. Imagine you're lifting your arm to wave a passing friend – this is the sort of speed at which you should lift the pole and strike into the fish, feeling a weighty knocking sensation as the fish is hooked and tries to escape.

Assuming the first fish you hook is quite small, under 2oz (or the size of your hand) – maybe it'll be a bright red-finned roach or rudd, or perhaps a stripy perch – you can land this without the aid of a landing net. Allow the fish to tire for a few seconds, using the flexible tip of the pole to absorb lunges, draw the fish towards where you're sitting and pick it up from the water, taking care to make sure your hands are wet so they don't damage the fish.

FIVE TO TRY

Churchgate Lakes
Churchgate Lakes, Rectory Road, Battlesbridge, Essex, SS11 7QR.
As seen on The Big Fish Off! Great lake for beginners and helpful staff.
01245 325289
enquiries@churchgatelakes.co.uk
www.churchgatelakes.co.uk

Makins Fishery
Bazzard Road, Bramcote, Nuneaton, Warwickshire, England, CV11 6QJ.
Lots of lakes to choose from and good facilities.
01455 220877
www.makinsfishery.co.uk

Marsh Farm Fishery
Hill Pond, Marsh Farm Fishery, Station Lane, Milford Surrey, GU8 5AE.
Great club-run water – give them a call for beginner's info.
01483 428885
godalming.angling@gmail.com
www.godalminganglingsociety.co.uk

White Acres
White Cross, Newquay, Cornwall, TR8 4LW.
Huge complex with something for everyone – great for a holiday.
01726 862100
www.news-reel.com

Partridge Lakes
Ribbon Lake, Culcheth, Warrington WA3 4AQ.
Fish-packed lakes and lots of species.
07469 981743
www.partridgelakes.co.uk

Ali runs Anna Kelle through a simlpe pole-fishing setup, baited with a single maggot.

Perch are often easy to catch - but be aware of their spikey dorsal fin and spines on the gill cover!

Please don't use a towel – most species (apart from perch) don't have spikes or spines and a gentle-but-firm grip is enough to prevent them from escaping as you take out the hook. If you do catch a perch, the spines on its back are obvious but it also has some on its gill plates (the hard area that covers the gill area) – however, these can't get you if you confidently grip its body in a wet hand so the head can't move, this way the sharp spikes on the gill covers aren't able to prick you. For species such as rudd and roach, which have no spines, teeth or spikes, simply maintain a firm-but-gentle grasp with a wet hand.

Unhooking your catch properly is important – you don't want to damage the fish in any way. A barbless hook is really easy to take out, just gently manoeuvre the hook back out the way it went in. If the fish is hooked a little further in the mouth, a plastic disgorger will help. You just position the line in the slot and move the disgorger down to the hook and push it out the way it went in. It may seem tricky at first so it's a good idea to get someone experienced to help, but practice makes perfect so don't be afraid to have a go once you've been shown how.

Now, all that remains is to carefully return the fish to the water. Congratulations – you've caught your first fish and you're now well on the way to becoming a Big Fish Off star! Remember to keep practicing your skills!

Catching your first fish is a great moment – enjoy the experience, treat your catch carefully and smile for the camera!

BEHIND THE SCENES

Ali had the task of teaching Anna Kelle how to fish from scratch – not an easy task in just a few hours – but the pair managed to amass a nice haul of roach and rudd using a simple pole rig and maggots as bait. However, Anna had a bit of trouble striking properly when the float indicated a bite, often not using enough force to pick up line and set the hook. This led to lots of missed bites and lost fish, ultimately costing Ali's team the challenge. It's fair to say that Ali wasn't best pleased with the result!

Once you've caught one fish, keep on feeding maggots regularly to keep the fish in the area and you'll be able to catch lots more. Also, the longer you feed the greater the chances of a bigger fish coming into your swim and picking up your hook bait. If you've been using one red or white maggot try two or even a grain of sweetcorn and you never know what size or species of fish you might hook next!

Now you've caught your first fish and you're familiar with the equipment and techniques, it's a good idea to practice as

Dean Macey perfected his skills catching lots of small fish on simple float tackle when he was young. Back then, he even had hair!

often as possible to keep improving your skills. For the first few years of Ali and Dean's fishing careers they did lots of this type of fishing at their local club waters and the skills they learnt then are still useful today.

Joining a club, as Ali and Dean did when they were learning, is a good idea at this stage. They'll often have small waters full of hungry fish that'll be easy to catch and some offer tuition for beginners, which will help you improve your skills. Your local tackle shop will be able to recommend a suitable club or search online for clubs in your area.

Once you've honed your skills catching smaller fish, it's time to tackle the larger species!

Although you may catch lots of different species in your first sessions, there are some common ones that you're very likely to encounter early in your angling career. Although you might catch small ones first, when larger these species are absorbing fish to target as you improve!

ROACH

These are probably the most common fish in the UK and they can top 4lb, but they're much more likely to be an ounce or two. They have bright steely silver scales with red fins. Generally, maggots are a great bait for roach of all sizes and they can be found in every type of canal, river, pond and lake. They usually feed near the bottom or a foot or two off it.

Roach are common across the UK and easy to catch when they're small – they love maggots, casters and bread.

RUDD

Very similar in appearance to the roach, rudd often have golden scales and bright red fins, compared to the roach's more subtle colours. Another good way to tell the two apart is by looking at the mouth – on a rudd it will be pointing upwards because the rudd loves feeding in the upper layers of slow-moving rivers, canals and lakes, whereas a roach's has a much more downward slant and pronounced 'overbite'. Larger rudd can be caught on bread, sweetcorn and maggots fished a foot or two below the surface and smaller ones will fall to the same tactics used for roach. A variant called golden rudd also exist and these are even brighter than normal rudd!

Rudd love feeding off the surface or in the upper layers of the water – check out the upward-pointing mouth.

PERCH

The spikey perch is a mini predator and loves devouring worms, maggots and even supermarket prawns and other fish! Easily identifiable with its striped body and large dorsal fin, they can grow to 6lb or more but one of a pound or more is a good specimen. They love hanging around cover such as weed beds, reeds, platforms, bridges, locks, trees and roots to ambush their prey but they're easily caught on a simple float rig with maggots or a section of worm - try a whole lobworm for a big one. Dawn and dusk are prime times for perch!

Perch are easily recognisable with their pronounced stripes and big dorsal fin – they're a great looking species.

Carp come in two main varieties – here's a mirror carp with patches of large scales. Common carp have scales all over.

CARP

The carp can grow to enormous sizes (we'll look at that further into the book as you gain more experience) and you may well catch some small ones when you're learning the basics - both Dean and Ali caught plenty of tiny carp during their Churchgate session. There are two main types; common carp with scales all over their bodies, and mirror carp with random patterns of small and large scales on an otherwise scale-free body. Carp can be greedy and will eat most things with maggots, pellets and sweetcorn real favourites. Try bread on the surface too!

THE BIG FISH OFF GUIDE TO FISHING

MONSTERS!
DEAN MACEY

Although many of the roach and rudd you'll catch might be small, they can both grow to an impressive size. Rudd, in particular, will often be bright gold in colour with scarlet fins – they're stunning creatures. Dean has caught some huge rudd and they're one of his favourite species: "A decent rudd or roach is a beautiful fish and one that I remember being incredibly excited to catch when I was a nipper. Big rudd, in particular, are spectacular and they're not too hard to catch. They love feeding in the upper layers and off the surface, so a small piece of bread pinched on the hook (known as breadflake) or a thumbnail-size piece of breadcrust on a simple float rig will catch them. But be prepared to use your eyes to spot them feeding or showing on the surface at dawn and dusk!" Here's Dean with a great example of a big rudd weighing 2lb 4oz, caught from a river in East Anglia using a tiny piece of bread and simple float fishing tactics. A great tip is to microwave a few slices of bread sealed in a sandwich bag for 30 seconds - this makes the bread stay on the hook much longer.

Dean with a monster rudd, which he stalked from an East Anglian river.

THE BIG FISH'O'FF GUIDE TO FISHING

CHAPTER 2 LEARNING TO USE A ROD & REEL

Now you've succeeded in learning the basics and catching plenty of smaller species on a whip, it's time to graduate to the next stage of your angling career. If you want to fish a little further out, in search of bigger fish, you'll need to learn how to use a rod and reel! Here's our advice...

Mark Bright and DJ Spoony get the lowdown from Ali on their rod-and-reel challenge.

You'll be able to use lots of skills you've learnt fishing with a whip, such as locating the fish and feeding the swim regularly, but you'll be able to cast further out to reach more fish and some different species. You'll also be able to land larger fish!

Starting with the tackle, a basic two or three-piece float rod teamed up with a small 2000-4000 size fixed-spool reel is an inexpensive option that will catch you lots of fish. This is just what ex-footballer Mark Bright and DJ Spoony used on their Big Fish Off adventure at Thames Water's Walthamstow Reservoir complex, where the teams faced off in a tense challenge using float rods, fixed-spool reels and float tactics on the complex's well-stocked junior lake.

SHOPPING LIST

If you've already got a basic whip set-up and some tackle, you can upgrade to a reel and line with the following sort of tackle. Younger anglers will appreciate a smaller rod and lighter reel whilst adults will be able to use a 12ft rod without any problems. Have a browse in a tackle shop and find out what feels comfortable.

- **Daiwa Harrier Match rod 10-13ft**
- **Fixed-spool reel 2000-4000 size**
- **5lb Pulse Line monofilament for main line**
- **Small selection of waggler floats**
- **Split shot in sizes SSG-No.8**
- **Size 18 ready-tied hooks to 3lb line**

Waggler floats are fixed bottom-end only and are perfect for use with a rod and reel because they cast well!

A fixed-spool reel is the most commonly used type of reel and features a stationary drum to hold the line and metal arm, called a bail arm, that rotates around the spool to load the line.

When you move the bail arm to one side, line can flow freely from the drum and this allows you to cast your rig. Moving the bail arm back again allows you to reel your line in.

FIVE TO TRY

For Life Experiences Fishing, Green Lane, Ampfield, Hampshire, SO51 9BN.
Designed to help the beginner. Go to flefishing.net or call 07595 024363.

Atkins Water, Waterbeach Road, Landbeach, Cambridgeshire, CB25 9FA.
Club-run day ticket water. www.waterbeachac.co.uk

Hampton Springs Fishery. Shay Lane, Hampton, Malpas, Cheshire, SY14 8AD.
Spring-fed series of lakes. Go to hamptonsprings.co.uk or call 01948 820789.

Twynersh Fishery, Thorpe Road, Chertsey, Surrey, KT16 9EJ.
Varied gravel-pit fishing. Check out twynershfishingcomplex.com or call 01932 570156.

Peterstone Coarse Lakes, St Brides Wentlooge, Newport, Wales, NP10 8SQ.
Picturesque complex of lakes full of interesting species! Call 01633 680905.

Casting is when you use the rod to propel the float and bait out into the lake or river – you disengage the bail arm, trap the line with your finger, move the rod back and then forwards vigorously to 'cast' the rig in the desired direction. The finger releases the line when the rod is pointing at an imaginary two-o'clock point. It's a good idea to practice this at a local playing field or park with plenty of room, using a small weight tied to the line and a target set 10-20m away to practice getting it right before you venture to the bank.

Adjusting the clutch allows you to dictate how much pressure a fish has to pull with before the reel gives line.

For best casting results, make sure that your reel is filled almost to the lip of the spool.

Back to the reel, the long number on the reel is a measurement used by tackle makers to identify the various sizes of reel, with 1000-4000 sizes suitable for float fishing, 4000-6000 angling for larger fish with heavier tackle and 6000 and above for big specimen carp and pike. A reel in the smaller category will be able to land surprisingly big fish so don't think you have to have a big reel to target the larger species.

All reels have a clutch – this is operated by a dial on the front of the spool or a knob on the rear, known respectively as front and rear drag reels. The clutch gives line from the spool under a certain pre-set pressure, which means a big fish can pull line off the reel instead of the line breaking. It makes a clicking sound when in operation and it's a good idea to set it so a sharp pull takes line straight off the spool before the hook length line would break, but not so loose that it comes into play when reeling in the rig.

It's important to match the reel size to the rod so they feel balanced and comfortable, try a few combinations at a tackle shop until you're totally happy.

They will also often help you put line on the reel too, and 5lb monofilament line is easy to use, strong and is quite elastic so it helps to cushion lunges from larger fish.

Ali changes the depth to keep the hook bait clear of weed and debris. This will make sure that the bait is presented where the fish can see it.

If you can't get someone to help you load the line onto your reel, it's easy to do it yourself too. Get a pencil and pierce the spool of line like a spindle, and thread the line through the bottom ring of your rod and tie onto the spool of the reel using a grinner knot, keeping the bail arm open. Now close the bail arm and start reeling to load the line, do this for a dozen meters and then stop to make sure the line isn't twisting as it comes off the spool, if it's twisted it'll curl up when you let it go slack. This isn't ideal and will cause problems when you're using it. Simply turn the spool around so the line is coming off the opposite way and it should stop twisting and load perfectly. Make sure your reel has a shallow spool that takes 100-200m of line and load it until the line is just below the lip of the front of the spool; about 1-2mm below is perfect. Most reels have a line clip on the side of the spool to secure the line so it doesn't peel off when not in use, but if yours doesn't then an elastic band will also work.

Urban wateres, such as the Thames Water-run Walthamstow Reservoirs, offer convenient access and well-stocked lakes.

DID YOU KNOW?

You can cast quite a long way with a rod, reel and float fishing tackle, maybe up to 30m with the right float, but casting is actually a discipline in itself with huge casting competitions taking place around the world. Using tackle more normally used in the sea, with long, stiff rods, special reels called multipliers loaded with extra thin line and big leads, the best casters can propel a 6oz weight over 900 feet, more than 270m!

Now you have your reel loaded with line, practice setting it up for a fishing session so you know how everything works. With the reel securely attached to the real seat on your rod, unclip the line and open the bail arm so the line is running out freely, and thread the line through the rings. It's fiddly so make sure you don't miss any or you'll have to start again! Let a rod-length of line out.

With the eyes threaded, take the end of the line, giving yourself plenty to play with, and thread on the float.

The best type of float to use for general float fishing is called a waggler. This is a simple stick shape with a bright tip that sits just above the water, a solid body and an eye at the end to run the line through. You'll have to shot the float correctly – this means using split shot to weigh the float down so just a centimetre or so of the bright tip sits proud of the water. You might remember how to attach split shot and how they work from the first chapter. The split shot also give the rig weight, which allows you to cast further out.

SPLIT SHOT CONVERSION CHART

SPLIT SHOT SIZE	WEIGHT	SHOT EQUIVALENT
SSG	1.6g	2 x AAA
AAA	0.8g	2 x BB
AB	0.6g	2 x No.1
BB	0.4g	2 x No.4
No.1	0.3g	2 x No.6
No.4	0.2g	2 x No.6
No.6	0.1g	
No.8	0.06g	

When shotting a waggler, it's important to remember that about three-quarters of the weight should be grouped around the float using a small number of large shot, this is called bulk shotting and it locks the float into place at the depth you want to fish at. You then use two or three much smaller shot down the line to sink the bait and hook slowly, so it mimics a bait falling naturally through the water.

Using the chart on this page and the weight rating written on the float, it's possible to work out what combination of shot you need to sink the float correctly.

For example, if your float was rated as 2 x SSG, you could use three AAA shot and a BB to lock the float, with two or three No.4 and No.6 shot strung out down the line. It's worth spending time to get just the right amount of shot so the float is nicely weighted down and indicates bites easily without the fish feeling the resistance.

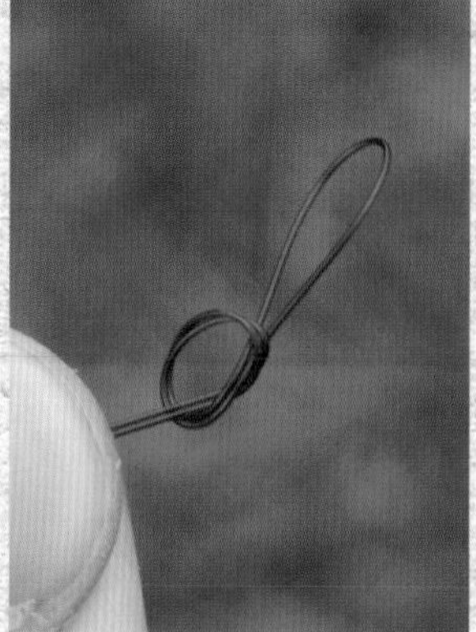

This is an overhand loop, which is perfect for attaching your main line to a pre-tied hook length.

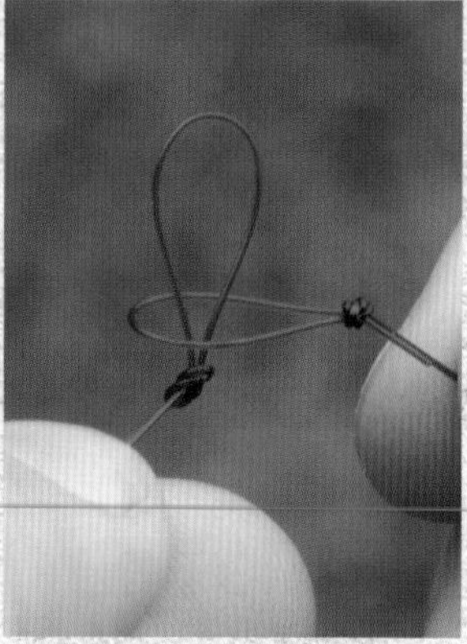

Pass the hook length loop through the main line loop then pop the hook through hook length loop and tighten.

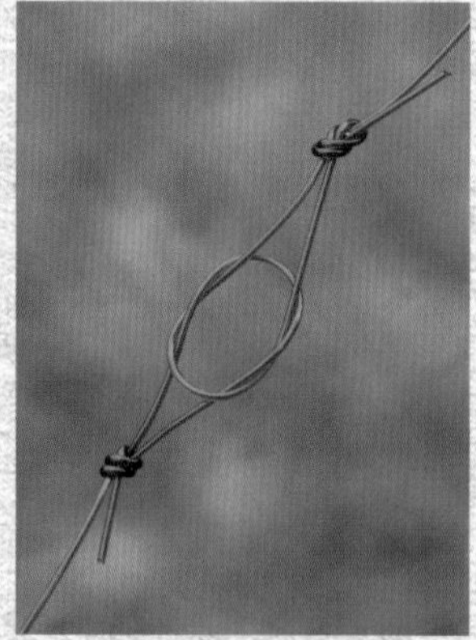

When you gently pull the two lines, the interlocking loops will draw down into a neat, strong connection.

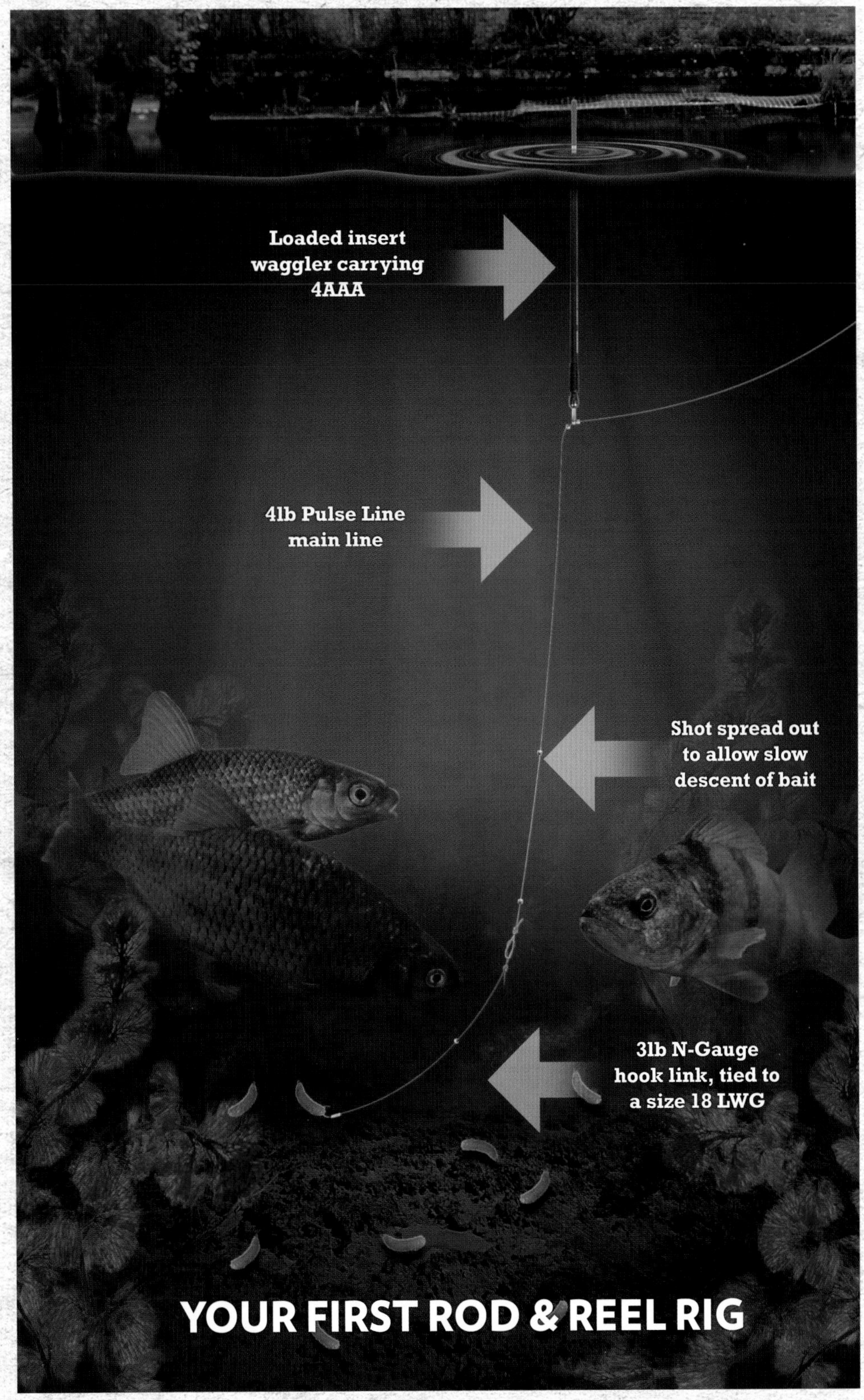

Loaded insert waggler carrying 4AAA

4lb Pulse Line main line

Shot spread out to allow slow descent of bait

3lb N-Gauge hook link, tied to a size 18 LWG

YOUR FIRST ROD & REEL RIG

Dean gets ready to net a larger fish for Brighty - but it's not the type of net the ex-Crystal Palace striker usually aims for!

BEHIND THE SCENES

The rod and reel challenge was plain sailing for Team Dean with Brighty on the rod catching plenty, but Ali and Spoony had a nightmare with the big weed bed in front of them. As Spoony wasn't great at casting, he kept on landing it in the weed so the float sat on the top and the bait was covered in weed. Dean and Brighty, however, found a clear area and set their float so the bait was presented above the weed and visible to the fish. Ali wasn't happy at losing this one!

To finish your rig, tie a simple overhand loop in the line below the float and use a loop-to-loop attachment for the ready-tied hook length, which is similar to the one you used when whip fishing first of all. With this attached, you're ready to go fishing!

Bait-wise, using a similar selection of coloured maggots as you did when whip fishing is a good bet for lots of fish and almost every species will eat them. Feed a few every few minutes and try single and double red or white maggots on the hook - a size 18 barbless model is deal.

Having chosen your venue, use the skills you learnt earlier on in your angling career to identify a suitable swim, making sure you have enough room to cast properly and the water in front of you is clear enough to fish in. With your rig set up and set to half of what you think the depth is, unleash those awesome casting skills you've been practicing and cast accurately to your chosen spot. Engage the bail arm to secure the line on the spool, take in some of the slack line without moving the float out of position and stay poised for a bite! Strike just as you did with the pole, in a firm-but-steady upward motion.

With the fish hooked, carefully guide it to the net. Don't let the line go slack or the fish will shake the hook out, with practice you'll be able to judge how much pressure to keep on but you won't break a 3lb hook length on smaller fish, under 1lb, easily.

Keep the loose-fed maggots going in every few minutes and it won't be long before you will hopefully encounter larger fish, which is when your reel and rod set up comes into its own. With the clutch on the reel able to give line and the rod absorb the lunges, fish much heavier than the breaking strain of your line can be landed.

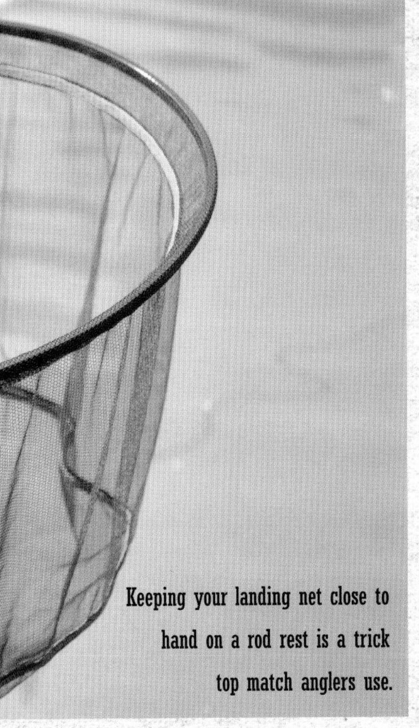

Keeping your landing net close to hand on a rod rest is a trick top match anglers use.

Species such as big perch, tench, carp and bream will put up a good scrap in the water, but by using the clutch you can tire the fish if you play it carefully. By guiding the fish away from any snags or obstacles, and using the rod's action to absorb the lunges of the fighting fish, you can tire and land even quite big fish on relatively light tackle. Why not watch an experienced angler for an hour to see how they play their fish? Once the fish has tired enough to allow you to guide it to the landing net, keep the rod up and as much line out as possible (don't wind in too much line, so the float and fish are close to the rod tip - keep both well apart!) and bring the net up once the fish is in over the top. Once the fish is in the net, keep it in the water while you make sure your unhooking mat is wet, your scales are ready and camera is to hand.

You can soon learn to catch a wider variety of species on a rod and reel. Why not see how many different species you can catch in a day for your very own Big Fish Off challenge?

A first session using a rod and reel at Walthamstow went well for Dean and stylish Brighty as he quickly picked up the knack of casting and feeding free offerings around his float to tempt the fish into the area, and his patience in watching the float was soon rewarded with a tench – a great looking fish with tiny green scales, big dark fins and small red eyes. They're a true English species and a favourite of many anglers. Brighty had a proper battle on his rod and reel to land the hard-fighting specimen and you can see how pleased he is from the pictures!

Spoony and Ali discuss tactics as the match hots up.

Brighty and Dean scorch into a 4-1 lead in the challenge!

A light catapult is perfect for accurately feeding maggots.

This type of small water is ideal for learning rod and reel basics and lots of similar venues are dotted up and down the country, often run by local angling clubs or as commercial fisheries. You can fish for the price of a day ticket or club membership, which can often be a cost-effective way of fishing fun waters like this if you go regularly.

Well-stocked lakes and ponds often hold a wide range of species and Dean's team caught tench, roach and even a trout! By setting the float at half of the estimated depth of the lake and feeding maggots and groundbait into the water, they drew fish to their hook bait and caught species they might not have done had they been fishing closer in with the whip. The clutch on the reel and longer rod also helped to absorb the lunges from the bigger fish so they tired and were able to be netted.

When you're fishing further out, it can be useful to have a special fishing catapult to fire bait out to where your float is, with some practice you can be really accurate and group the loose feed maggots or pellets tightly around the float for maximum attraction.

This way you can feed much further than you can throw the bait, which allows you to fish and feed in much deeper water away from the bank where more fish will be present.

Taking a wide selection of baits means that you can tempt whichever species happens to be feeding.

By fishing this way, you're likely to catch a wide range of species including perch, roach, rudd, bream, tench and even carp, plus you'll expand your angling skills further. Fishing with a rod and reel is a really satisfying way of catching lots of fish and watching a float is great fun!

Once you've become confident with catching a variety of smaller species on your rod and reel, it's time to raise the bar a little and tackle some larger fish and the slightly trickier fishing methods needed to tempt them.

Tench love to hide amongst marginal weed, in a host of venue types from tiny farm ponds to gravel pits.

Dean and Mark Bright with a fine tench - check out the small red eye.

TENCH

Also known as the Doctor Fish, the tench is a fine looking fish with a green body, ranging from bright olive to nearly black, and a small red eye. They're a member of the carp family and usually feed on or near the bottom, with a particular eye for maggots, worms, sweetcorn and bread flake.

They love weed beds and lily pads, so present a bait near or on the bottom around these areas and a fine tench could be yours!

THE BIG FISH OFF GUIDE TO FISHING

MONSTERS!
DEAN MACEY

Dean loves using a rod and reel to catch all sorts of fish, and perch are one of his favourites during the winter months when they're at their most colourful. This specimen weighed 3lb 2oz and was caught on a simple float fishing rig, fixed-spool reel and float rod – maybe you'll hook something similar one day?

Tench are a really interesting species and they can grow to some considerable size given the right diet and water conditions. Being a summer species, they thrive in hot weather and feed voraciously at dawn and dusk, making pinprick bubbles appear on the surface as they grub around the bottom for food. Dean has caught some giant tench, including this monster of 10lb 12oz! But any tench over 5lb is a fine fish and the females, identifiable by their smaller fins compared to the male's larger, spoon-like pelvic fins, grow the largest.

Dean with a massive tench of well over 10lb, a true specimen.

Big perch are really impressive fish and ideal targets on simple float fishing tactics on a rod and reel.

DAIWA

CHAPTER 3 TARGET BIGGER FISH

Now you've gained experience in targeting different species on a rod and reel and pole, it's time to take the step up to targeting larger fish and bigger species on more advanced float fishing tactics. It's great fun on a mixed-stock water as you don't know what species or size of fish you're going to catch when the float goes down!

You'll be using all the basic skills you've learnt in previous chapters but you'll be have to be extra cunning to land the bigger fish – if Razor Ruddock can be quiet enough to not scare them off, you'll have no problem!

Maybe your club or local tackle shop run a small or medium size water with a mix of species to target, or a local fishery has a mixed-species lake? This would be a perfect location to test your skills further, just like the teams did on their visit to the Cricket Pit near Colchester, Essex. Ali fished here a lot when he was a kid and the skills he learnt here are ones he uses lots in his fishing to this day.

Ali and Dean line up with their partners, Neil 'Razor' Ruddock (second right) and Steve Collins (right) at Essex club water the Cricket Pit. Their target species were tench and bream, and lots of them!

Ali cut his teeth on the Cricket Pit, catching mixed bags plus some bigger specimens so it was a homecoming of sorts!

In previous chapters, we've gone through fishing up in the water and catching smaller fish on maggots and other simple baits. This is fine for smaller fish but now you've gained experience with fish of this size, it's time to tackle some larger specimens.

By tweaking your tactics slightly and using more advanced rigs and techniques, you'll be able to specifically target the larger bream, tench, perch and carp, as well as bigger samples of fish you've caught before, such as roach and rudd.

During the boy's session on the Cricket Pit, they encountered some big bream and tench, with both Razor Ruddock and Steve Collins having to learn new skills to fish for them. But it's not that difficult – you just need to practice and make sure you're using the correct equipment.

FIVE TO TRY

Sumners Ponds Fishery, Chapel Road, Barns Green, West Sussex, RH13 0PR.
This pretty fishery has something for every level of experience. Go to www.sumnersponds.co.uk or call 01403 732539 for more.

Cricket Pit, Colchester Postal & Telecom Angling Club, Kellers Lane, Wivenhoe, Essex.
Where Ali honed his angling skills and the scene of Razor Ruddock and Steve Collins' float fishing challenge. Go to www.cptac.co.uk or email info@cptac.co.uk

Alvechurch Fisheries, Bittell Road, Birmingham, B45 8BW.
A great mixed fishery. Check out www.alvechurch-fisheries.co.uk or call 0121 4454274 for details.

River Thames, Oxfordshire, Berkshire and Surrey.
This big, slow-moving river holds lots of species and you'll be able to use float fishing tactics.

Bradshaw Hall Fisheries, Bolton, Lancashire, BL2 4JW.
Nine lakes to choose from and an on-site cafe over 50 acres. Go to www.bradshawhallfisheries.co.uk

Dean and Steve watch their float for signs of fish or a bite. Even the slightest twitch is enough to get the pulse racing.

The first thing to do when you arrive at the lake or fishery, is to find an ideal spot to fish from. Your eyes are your best weapon for this part of the day and a good set of polarised sunglasses and a hat will help you make out signs of fish and suitable fish-holding areas to fish near – weedbeds, reeds, depth changes and overhanging trees all provide homes for fish of all species. Make sure you're there at dusk or dawn as this is when most fish like to be active and show themselves.

Larger fish will also show themselves by bubbling – this occurs when they're feeding on the bottom and expelling small air bubbles from their gills. Bream and tench will often feed in this way at dawn and dusk and you can work out where they like to feed by watching for these signs. They'll also come to the surface and 'roll' with their backs out of the water sometimes. Carp also like to do this and you'll often see them on the surface when it's warm, and when they feed they'll give off larger bubbles.

Colchester PTAC run the Cricket Pit in Essex - it's an ideal venue for some more advanced float fishing tactics.

By looking for these signs and working hard to find where the fish are, you'll be able to work out the best place to fish.

DID YOU KNOW?

Pole fishing in the modern form with an elasticated section attached to the line was a French invention with the idea quickly spreading throughout Europe and the UK in the 70s, 80s and 90s. Modern carbon poles utilise space-age technology and can be up to 16m long. They can be really expensive due to the high quality carbon fibre used in construction – a top-of-the-range 16m Daiwa Air XLS model costs nearly £4,000! But, thankfully, you'll be able to find a perfectly usable model for around £100 and tackle shops will elasticate the top sections for you for a modest fee, making it easy to set up.

Once you've found a good swim, you'll have to choose which method you're going to use. For The Big Fish Off, Dean and Steve chose to use a rod and line, just like you've been using. They only needed to use slightly heavier line and a bigger hook for the larger bait and fish.

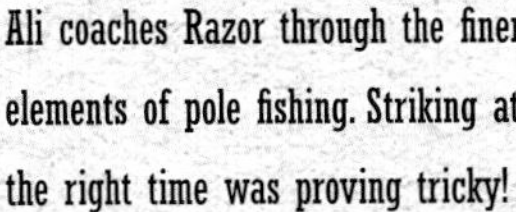

Ali coaches Razor through the finer elements of pole fishing. Striking at the right time was proving tricky!

Dean talks Steve, a non-angler, through the rod and reel setup he'll be using.

Ali and Razor decided on a different tactic – an elasticated pole. This is similar to the whip you used when starting out but it has a length of elastic running through the top two or three sections of the pole. This helps to cushion the runs and lunges from a larger fish, in the same way that soft rod will do. Different strength of elastics can be used for different sizes of fish and you can land surprisingly big fish on a pole set up in this way.

Razor was using a simple pole rig set to fish a bait on the lake bed, where the bigger fish will be more likely to feed. An area near to a weedy marginal shelf was a great choice of swim too as this will hold lots of natural food, attracting species such as bream, carp and tench.

Ready-tied pole rigs are a trouble-free option.

Dean's simple waggler rig for larger fish. He grouped much of the split shot down the line to sink the bait to the lake bed quickly.

Next door, Dean's team opted for a waggler float rig, again set to full depth. Using more weight down the line made sure the hook bait went to the bottom quickly, avoiding the smaller species and helping to keep the float stable.

Both teams used rigs similar to the ones you've used before, but instead of fishing midwater, you'll have to work out the depth using a plummet – a small weight that attaches to the end of the line and indicates if your float is set too deep, too shallow or just right to be fishing with your bait on the bottom.

SHOPPING LIST

- A selection of wagglers
- Size 18 or 16 MWG hooks
- Selection of split shot
- Unhooking mat
- Scales
- Sweetcorn
- Maggots
- Groundbait
- Plummet

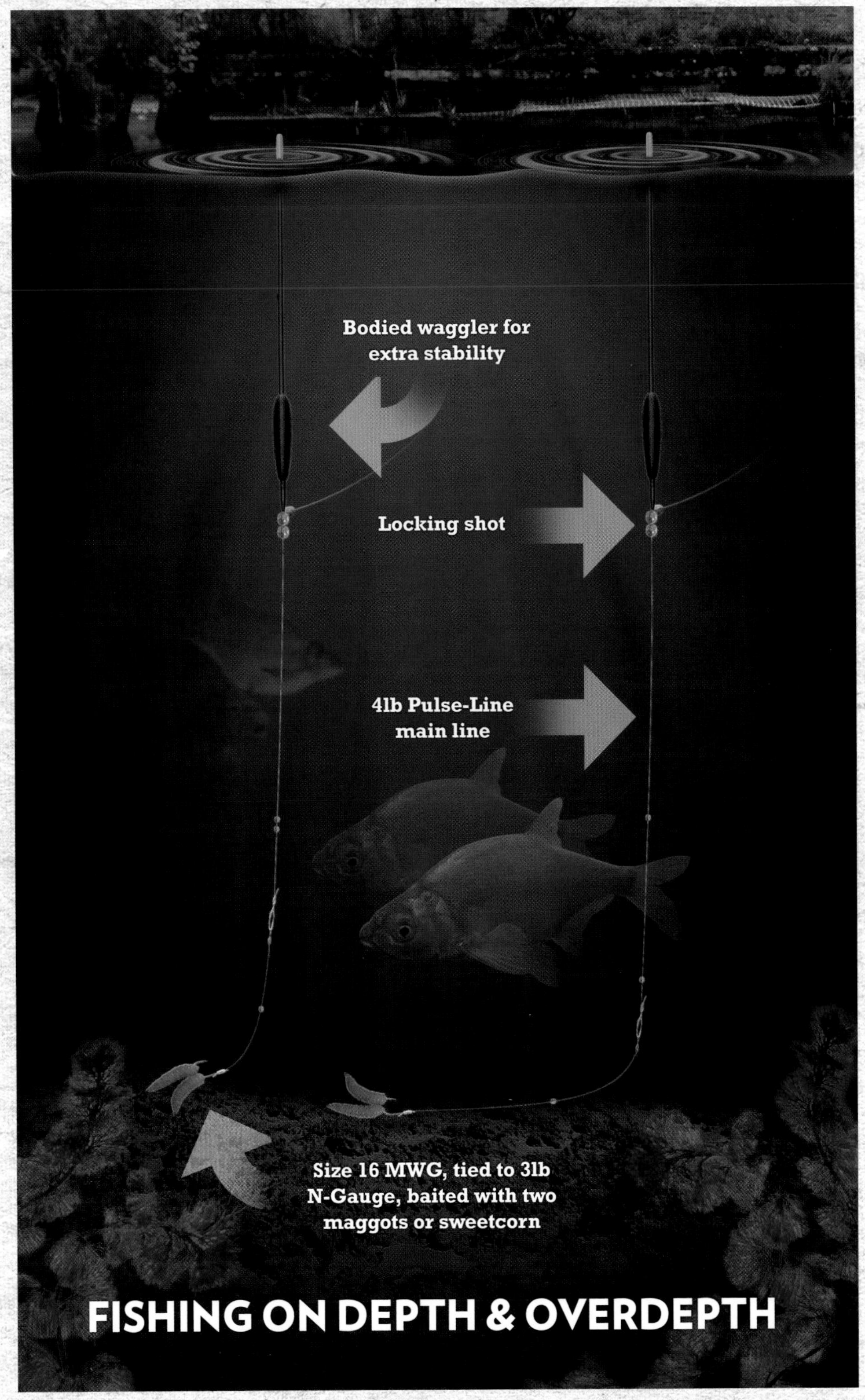

Bodied waggler for extra stability

Locking shot

4lb Pulse-Line main line

Size 16 MWG, tied to 3lb N-Gauge, baited with two maggots or sweetcorn

FISHING ON DEPTH & OVERDEPTH

Dean shows Steve how to perfect the art of patience!

As well as maggots, both teams opted to use groundbait – this a crumb-like powder containing lots of things fish love to eat. When you wet the crumb and compress the groundbait into balls, you can throw it into your swim, where it'll break down in the water and send attractive smells and tastes into the water to get the interest of passing fish. Don't use too much – three or four tangerine-sized balls will be enough to start with, with a top up of two or three more balls every hour or so. You can also loose feed maggots with your catapult. Being accurate is important so all your feed ends up in the same area and concentrates the fish where you're casting.

As before, staying patient and being accurate with your casting and feeding is important and with any luck, you'll soon have some nice fish feeding on your spot. You've already become experienced in identifying bites and striking, so stay alert and use the clutch and cushioning action of the rod, or the pole elastic, to wear the fish out before bringing it to the net.

Remember to stay on guard if you have snags the fish can get in – you don't want to lose your first bigger fish!

An unhooking mat is a useful accessory as it prevents the fish from laying on the hard ground when you have it on the bank. It's essential for larger species such as carp so you can return them without damage. Fish care is vital and, as any angler will tell you,

Razor Ruddock had a battle royale on light pole tackle with this bream but the elastic did its job of cushioning the fish's runs.

taking good care of your catch is important. Keep the fish wet by wetting nets, slings and mats in the margins before using.

With the knowledge and experience you now have of targeting different species and sizes of fish on two different types of tackle, you'll be able to go to bigger waters and enjoy catching lots of different species!

A commercial-style water (a fishery that is stocked and run profit) is a good next step, once you've honed your skills, because it offers larger fish still, including larger carp, which will test your tackle to the limit, plus species you've already encountered. You can use new tactics too but the principles you've learnt so far on your Big Fish Off adventure will still be useful as you tackle the next challenge.

BREAM

The slab-sided bream lives in shoals with others of a similar size and will eat most things, particularly small, smelly baits such as a section of worm, maggots or grain of sweetcorn. The bream has a very flat body so it can move around in tight shoals easily and can grow to over 20lb, but is normally a few ounces or pounds, with a good bream over 5lb and a massive one 10lb-plus. They don't fight very hard but they can appear in large numbers once you have a shoal in your swim!

Steve and Dean with a chunky tench that put up a great fight on rod and line! You can use many of the same tactics that you would for bream.

Razor was rightly proud of this sizeable bream.

This makes the bream a great target species - it's possible to catch lots in one session with bags totalling over 100lb possible.

They're the sheep of the underwater world! To target a big bag of bream, plenty of bait is often required but it doesn't have to be expensive. Kilo bags of sweetcorn from the supermarket cost a pound and some bags of basic brown crumb from a tackle shop can be mixed with water and made into groundbait balls to throw into your swim. Add the sweetcorn and juices to the groundbait along with a few maggots or some hempseed to really tempt the greedy bream! Creating a carpet of food in this way will hold bream and species like tench and carp in your swim as they graze the bottom, enabling an angler to catch multiple fish in one session.

If you're really keen, why not go to your chosen water the night before fishing and bait your swim before fishing the next morning - this is called pre-baiting and it's a reliable way of ensuring there are fish in your swim when you arrive to fish.

THE BIG FISH OFF GUIDE TO FISHING

MONSTERS!

The teams caught plenty of nice bream up to 5 or 6lb in their challenge, but these greedy bottom-feeding fish can grow much larger and the record stands at nearly 23lb now! The giant pictured here, caught by British carp angler Mark McKenna, weighed 22lb 9oz, and held the record in 2012. Any bream over 10lb is considered to be an exceptional specimen.

A pole isn't just for small fish – equipped with some powerful elastic to cushion the runs of big fish, a strong pole can land monster-sized fish! This 132lb wels catfish, caught by a French angler in 2014, is the largest fish ever caught on a pole and put up a titanic 30-minute battle attached to a 13m pole and 150lb braided line, almost dragging the daredevil angler into the lake!

Think the pole is just for small fish? Think again! This 132lb catfish was banked on one, making it the biggest freshwater fish landed on a pole!

This huge bream once held the British record! Carp angler, Mark Mckenna caught it from a Cambridgeshire stillwater. What an awesome specimen!

CHAPTER 4
BAG UP ON COMMERCIALS

Commercial fisheries are a relatively new type of angling venue, but have already become hugely popular amongst match and pleasure anglers. Their creation came as a result of anglers wanting to be able to fish on venues that were comfortable and had good facilities, and where they were pretty much guaranteed action, often from hard-fighting species such as carp, tench or our old friend, the bream.

Often these venues will be a complex of small lakes that have been purpose-dug to provide the perfect environment for a large number of anglers to go and bag up! Normally carp will be one of the main species they contain – usually single-figure and double-figure fish but in large numbers – but generally there will be a good variety of other fish as well, including roach, perch, tench, bream and F1s (a type of carp hybrid).

Commercials have grown massively in terms of popularity and now attract large numbers of anglers, with venues all over the country, and new ones springing up all the time, to the extent that far fewer people can be found on rivers and canals, compared to bygone years.

Increased competition has meant that these fisheries are offering more than ever before in terms of the variety of species, including ones that you would normally associate with rivers such as barbel and chub, as well as high stocking levels to ensure year-round action, plus facilities such as onsite tackle shops. They can be fished on a day ticket, so you can literally turn up in the morning, grab breakfast in the café; get all the tackle and bait you need for the day, plus some advice on how best to use it, in the onsite tackle shop; and then go and set up in your chosen peg, fully expecting some quick action.

Large fisheries such as Cudmore in the Midlands often consist of several lakes of varying size and shape.

Whilst fishing commercial venues, you might encounter some new fishes such as the crucian and common carp hybrid known as an F1.

This makes commercials the perfect place for newcomers to our sport, as you can actually go along and catch plenty, even if your techniques and tackle are fairly basic, plus you can watch and learn from other anglers around you.

Some venues even have onsite coaches that you can book to teach you!

This type of venue was the perfect place for The Big Fish Off team to take Sally Gunnell and Anna 'AK' Kelle for their first attempts at fishing. The pair started off on Churchgate Lakes to get an idea of the basics and caught load of roach, rudd and small carp on the pole. They then moved onto Gloucester Park, and both Sally and AK ended up catching carp to double-figures, under the expert tuition of Dean and Ali. Spoony and Mark Bright also tackled a commercial fishery called Lake John, in Hertfordshire, and caught lots of carp and bream.

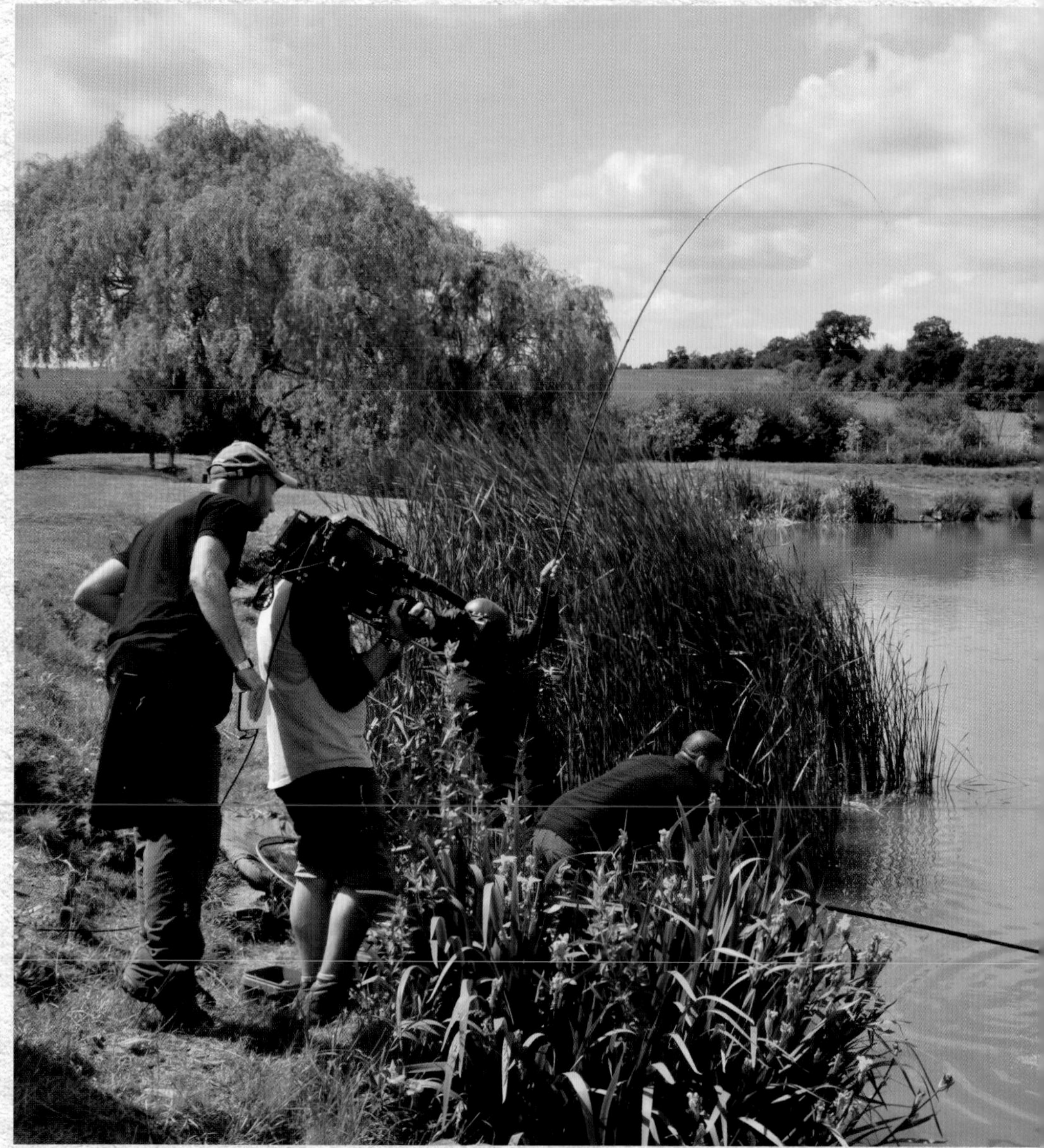

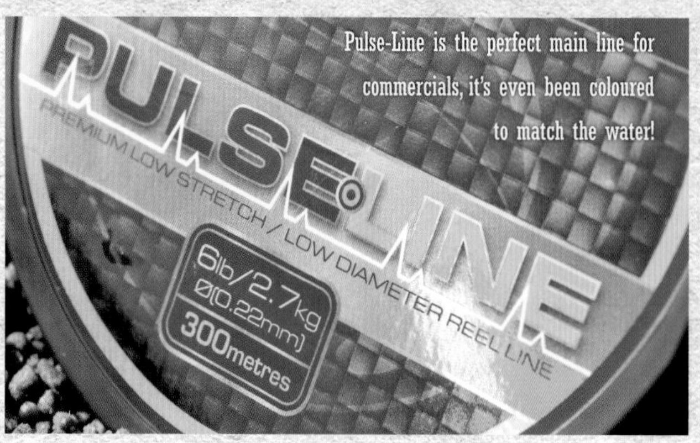

Pulse-Line is the perfect main line for commercials, it's even been coloured to match the water!
PULSE LINE
PREMIUM LOW STRETCH / LOW DIAMETER REEL LINE
6lb/2.7kg
Ø(0.22mm)
300metres

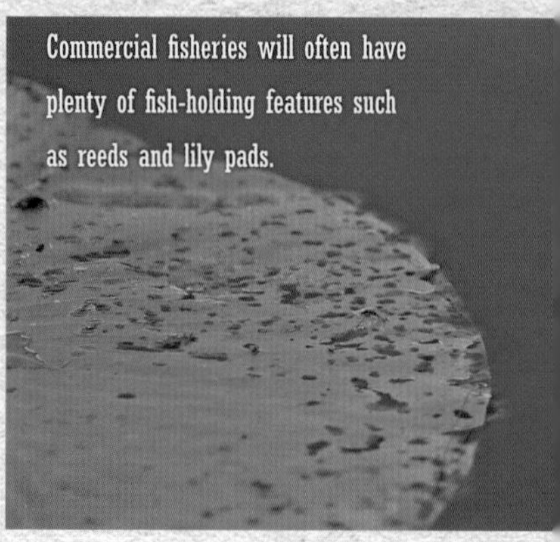
Commercial fisheries will often have plenty of fish-holding features such as reeds and lily pads.

FIVE TO TRY

Cudmore Fishery, Newcastle-under-Lyme, Staffordshire, ST5 5HW.
Masses of different species!
Call 01782 680919.

Lake John, Waltham Abbey, Essex.
The one for big match weights.
Call 07958 938153.

Woodland Lakes, Thirsk, North Yorkshire, YO7 4NJ.
13 lakes to choose from!
Call 07831 824870.

Magiscroft, Cumbernauld, Scotland, G67 4AF.
Seven lakes and over 150 swims.
Call 01236 737577 for more info.

Willinghurst Fisheries, Shamley Green, Surrey.
The 11-lake complex for all anglers. Call 07774 188760 or go to www.willinghurstfishery.co.uk for further details.

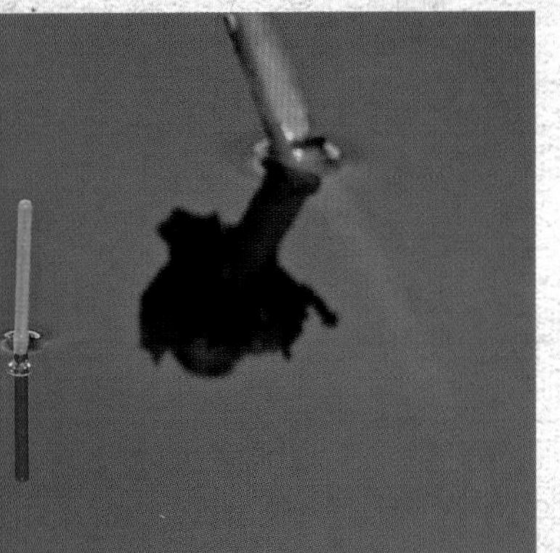

Ali and Spoony had some fast-paced action with lots of good-sized fish – just what commercials are all about.

TACKLE

The popularity of commercial fisheries has led to tackle being developed that is specifically designed for this type of water. Due to their size and fact that you usually won't be fishing far out, there isn't really any need for the longer rods that you will see people using on bigger lakes and rivers – especially when it comes to those designed for float fishing.

Whereas a traditional float rod tended to be 12, 13 or even 14ft, most of those designed for commercials are only 10ft or 11ft in length. They will also have a very different action, as they often need to be able to handle carp, so will have a stiffer action. The same is true when it comes to rods used for feeder fishing, which will be very different to that which you would typically use on a river.

Any smaller sized fixed spool reel is suitable as long as it has a good drag and decent cranking power – there is no need for the spool to hold huge amounts of line as you aren't going to be fishing at longer range If you are targeting carp then you are going to want a main line of 6-10lb in breaking strain, or 3-4lb is sufficient if you are fishing for smaller species such as roach, bream and rudd..

When it comes to floats, wagglers in the 2BB to 3AAA range will cover most situations for general fishing, or if you're specifically targeting carp then a loaded waggler is ideal.

These are weighted floats to give the weight needed to cast the required distance accurately, whilst allowing you to fish without any shot down the line so your hook bait can sink slowly, and fish will take it on the drop.

Method feeders (right) and Hybrid feeders (below) are a quick and easy way of tackling a multitude of species on well-stocked fisheries.

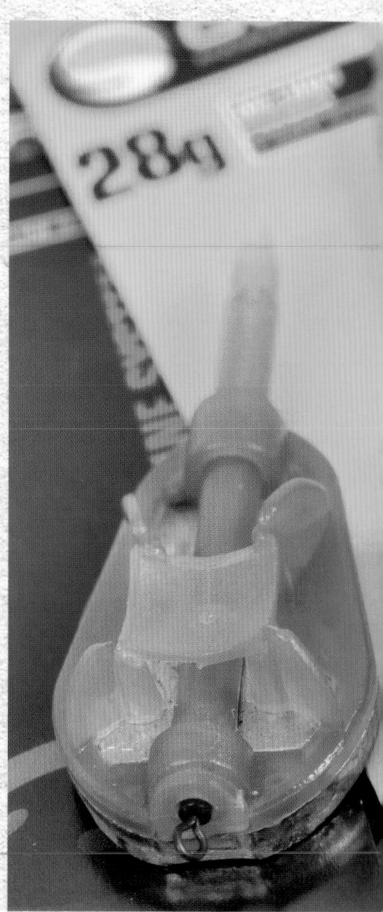

Another very effective way of float fishing on many commercials is to use a pole, and usually you don't need to fish far out. A pole allows you to fish very accurately, especially to features, and gives great presentation, and the ones available these days are very lightweight, and you won't need to to break the bank to buy one. You can tie your own rigs from scratch, but there are plenty of good ready-tied ones available that are suitable for everything from catching small roach to targeting double-figure carp. You will need to choose an elastic that is strong enough to land the fish that you are targeting, but not so stiff that you bump fish on the strike. Plenty of heavy ones, like Black Hydro, which is designed for hauling carp, are available.

For feeder fishing, by far the most popular way of fishing is to use either a pellet feeder or Method feeder.

There are also times though when fishing with a PVA bag filled with baits such as pellets can be very effective, or even just a straight lead and catapulting a few free offerings around it, especially if the fish have become wary of finding small piles of bait that often result with them getting a hook in their mouth when they eat them!

This style of fishing was actually invented on commercial fisheries and is incredibly effective, especially for carp, but also other species as well. It is basically a way of fishing your hook bait right in amongst a small pile of groundbait and free offerings, such that a fish will come along and pick up your bait along with everything else without even realising it is attached to a hook until it is too late and it has hooked itself!

Method feeders themselves have changed a lot over the years and used to be quite big, cumbersome and awkward to load properly. That has all changed now though with the advent

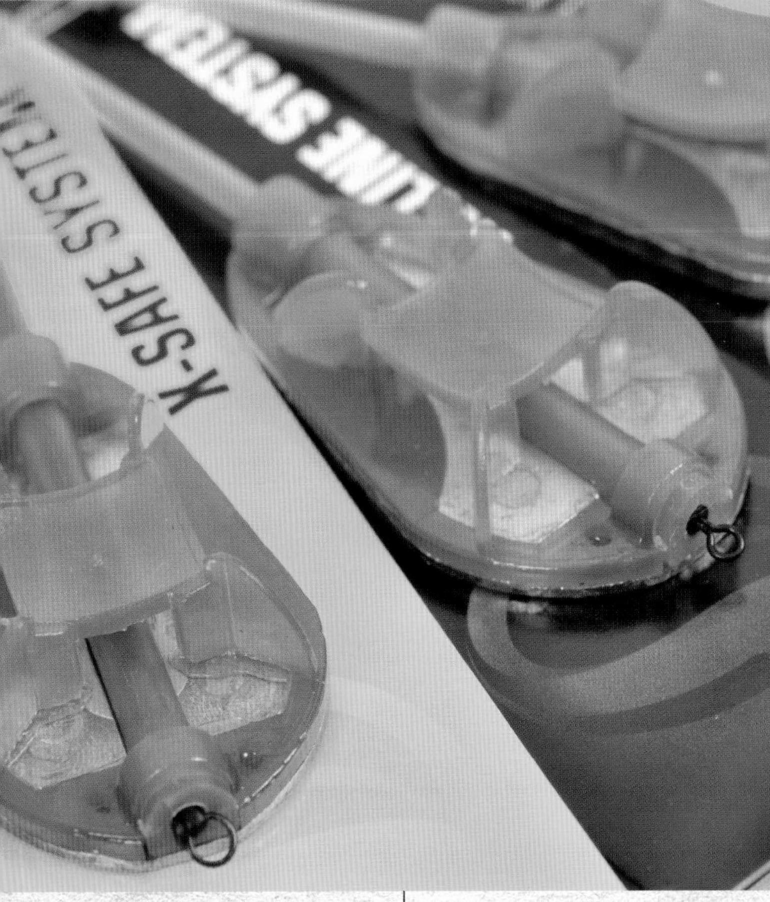

TOP TIP

A Method-style feeder allows you to desposit a neat pile of bait on the bottom with your hook bait right at the centre, ensuring feeding fish will suck it up and hook themselves. To correctly load this type of feeder, place the hook bait onto the central platform and mould damp micro pellets around it to form a neat parcel. Use the same proecdure for the Hybrid feeder but with the hook bait positioned near the surface under a layer of pellets. Companies such as Guru make dedicated moulds to use with their Method feeders, which make baiting up easy.

of flat Method feeders that come with a purpose designed 'mould' that you simply fill with groundbait, place your hookbait in, and then press the feeder into, and you're all ready to cast out! The latest evolution of this feeder is called the Hybrid and is even easier to use and more effective.

They can be fished with a variety of hookbaits – either directly on the hook or on a hair rig - and a short hook length, which creates a bolt rig so that the fish hook themselves. These feeders tend have an attachment which allows you to quickly change your hook link, as the fishing on these venues can be hectic at times!

This way of fishing is now incredibly popular as it is so easy to do, and very effective on many waters, where you can turn up and lob out a Method feeder and be in with a good chance of catching. It has spawned a variety of terminal tackle, and even rods, purpose-designed for this type of fishing.

OTHER METHODS

If you are targeting the carp, especially in venues that hold bigger fish, then standard specimen carp tactics can also work well. Often the action will be fairly hectic and you'll be fishing in such a way as to try and get bites quickly.

This is likely to include using brightly coloured hookbaits and boosting them with a liquid attractor, such as Goo, to help carp home in on them faster.

One of the great things about commercials is the variety and size of fish – Ali and Spoony were delighted with this fin-perfect mirror carp.

Top Right: Small, bright hook baits are winners on well-stocked waters – it pays to carry a selection!

You can also catch plenty of carp on these venues by fishing with a float, or more specifically, a pellet waggler. These loaded floats have been specially designed for fishing with a pellet hookbait and for targeting carp that are feeding in the upper layers, well off of the bottom. The idea is basically to keep loosefeeding pellets on a little-and-often basis to get the carp interested and competitively taking freebies as they sink through the water. You then fish your pellet waggler over the top, with a hookbait that sinks naturally, and the carp will take the bait on the drop. Part of the challenge is to find at what depth the fish are most readily taking the bait and then set your hook link length accordingly, as this will bring quicker bites.

The float is also very effective for other species, but often the hardest thing is to get your hook bait down to the bottom where it is likely to be picked up by species such as tench, bream and crucian carp. The numbers of small roach and rudd in these venues can make that difficult and it is a good idea to fish a fairly heavy waggler, which will take enough bulk shot, that you can put this 12 inches or so from your hook to ensure that it sinks quickly. Bigger baits can also help, and if there are a lot of small fish in the upper layers it is best to avoid feeding baits such as maggots, which drive them into a frenzy.

A hair-rigged pellet allows plenty of room for the carp to prick itself on the exposed hook when it sucks in the tasty morsel.

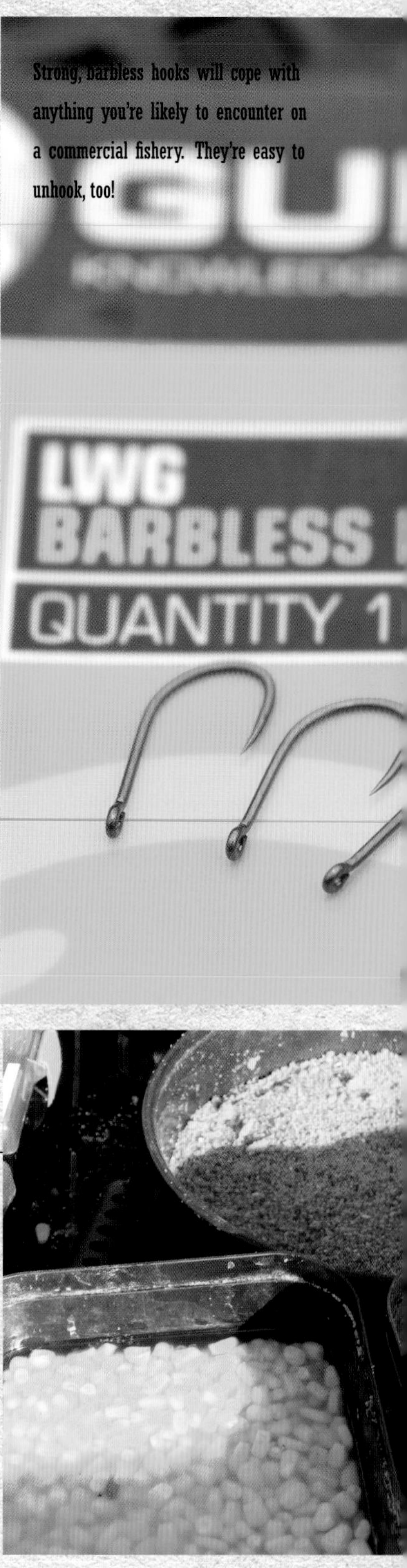

Strong, barbless hooks will cope with anything you're likely to encounter on a commercial fishery. They're easy to unhook, too!

Pellets are by far the most popular bait on this type of venue, and can also help when it comes to picking out the bigger fish.

The fish in these lakes will have come from a fish farm, which will have used pellets to feed them on and are something that the fish will have eaten all of their lives, and so pretty much recognise them as a natural source of food!

A huge variety of different pellets is available, but on many of these waters they only allow the use of ones with lower oil content, or even have their own type of pellet that you have to use. Typically you would feed hard pellets straight out of the bag and then either attach one of those to the hook using a latex bait band, or use one that has been softened so that you can put a hook through it or fish it on a hair rig. Soft pellets can be bought in a wide variety of flavours, colours and sizes, or you can prepare your own using expander pellets and a bait pump.

BEHIND THE SCENES

During the filming of the Spoony and Mark Bright episode, the teams had a constant companion in the form of Spoony's dog Duke, who followed the teams throughout their various challenges. Although he was immaculately behaved, Duke wasn't impressed with their antics and spent most of time laying around asleep or totally disinterested. Even dog lover Ali couldn't get Duke to pay attention, showing fishing isn't for everyone!

Simple baits will often work well on mixed-stock lakes – casters, corn and ground bait for making into small balls to feed the swim with are all good bets.

Traditional baits such as maggots and casters (the chrysalis form of the maggot) will work on these venues, but often they will attract too much attention from small fish, which these lakes are often teeming with!

Meat is a good alternative – such as tinned luncheon meat – and can be deadly when fished in cubes for species such as carp and tench. Sweetcorn can also work well, as will mini boilies in various colours and flavours, but with any of these waters you will need to check exactly what the rules allow you to use. A size 16 hook is a good all-round option for such baits, as it allows you to fish one or two grains of corn or a small cube of meat, which will attract a host of bottom-feeding species.

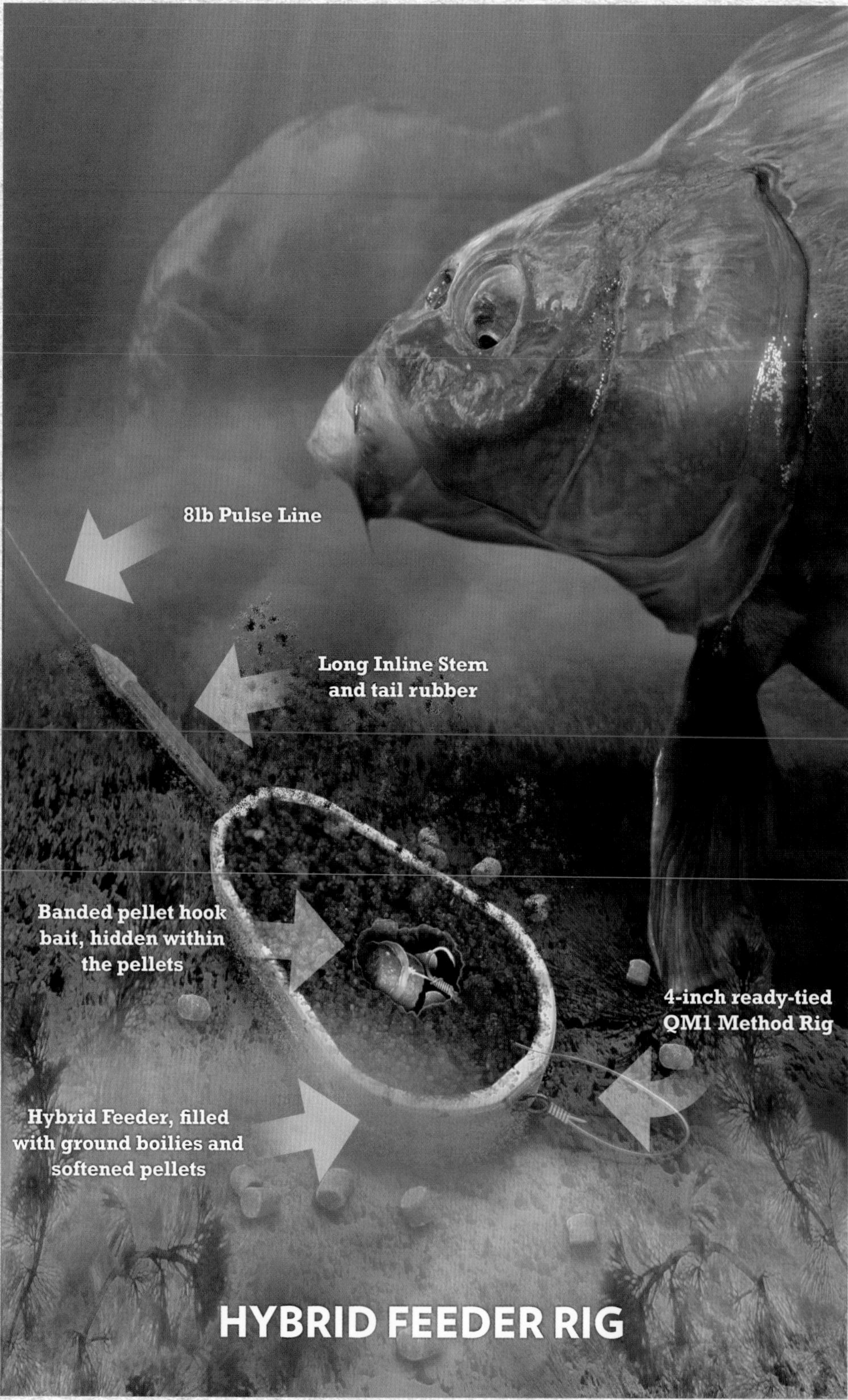
8lb Pulse Line
Long Inline Stem
and tail rubber
Banded pellet hook
bait, hidden within
the pellets
4-inch ready-tied
QM1 Method Rig
Hybrid Feeder, filled
with ground boilies and
softened pellets
HYBRID FEEDER RIG

Ali cast his bait-laden Hybrid feeder tight to the island in front of his team's swim, and it wasn't long before Spoony was playing this bream to the net. They're a common species in commercial fisheries.

DID YOU KNOW?

Commercial fisheries are very popular with match anglers and produce some huge weights, as well as big payouts for the winner, with prizes topping £25,000 in some cases! There are now waters that are so highly stocked that many of the anglers taking part in matches on them will end up landing over 100lb of fish in five hours, usually mostly made up of carp, whereas in years gone by that sort of weight would easily have been enough to win. We are now at the stage where 1,000lb is possible, certainly in a six-hour match, and this was proven by well-known match hauler Gary Huth. In 2014 Gary set a new record at Aaron's Lake, in Essex, when he landed a staggering 977lb of carp during a six hour match – that was around 220 fish landed and equated to him putting one in his net roughly every 100 seconds! More usually, any bag approaching triple figures – like the one shown over the page with Adam Rooney, is worth shouting about!

Although these waters are often very highly stocked, there will still be areas that the fish prefer to frequent. Because many of these lakes are man-made there is often little in the way of underwater features, but in general the lake bed will be pretty flat where it has been scooped out with a digger.

The main features tend to be the margin shelf, especially if there is also any sort of cover for the fish such as reed beds or overhanging trees, or the margins of any islands.

Fishing close in can be very good at times, especially in the evenings when these lakes can often be a bit quieter, plus many anglers throw their unused bait in when they pack up, and the fish are used to finding free food in the edge at the end of the day!

But often when the lakes are busy and there is a lot of disturbance the fish will push further out, making island margins the perfect feature to fish to, as species such as carp will definitely patrol around them. These venues tend to be shallow anyway, often averaging 3-4ft, so during the warmer months don't be afraid to try fishing in just a foot or so of water, especially as these lakes are usually coloured. Overhanging bushes or reed beds on the island can act as 'fish magnets', especially if the rest of the bank is fairly bare.

You can accumulate a seriously big weight of fish during a day or five-hour match on some commercial fisheries – here's top match angler Adam Rooney with part of a huge haul of carp!

Fishing to an island can present its own problems if you want your rig to land in the water as opposed to on the bank or up a tree! This is where the line clip on your reel comes in handy – simply cast aiming to land short of the island, then pull off some extra line and clip-up, and keep repeating until you are clipped up at the right distance.

The clip will prevent you from overcasting, but make sure you keep the rod in the same position every time you cast and whilst you wait for the clip to be hit.

A line clip is a great aid in fishing accurately.

Bream can be big weightbuilders too – they often travel in large shoals and are reliable back-up species if the carp aren't feeding.

In many situations you can leave the line in the clip once you're cast out and fishing, as the fish will come towards you when hooked as they have nowhere else to go, but be ready to quickly unclip if you hook something bigger that decides to tear off down the lake!

If the island is fairly close to the bank then this is where pole fishing can really come into its own, as it allows you to fish very tight to it, without having to worry about losing rigs if you mis-cast!

Jim Mathews shows the potential of commercials for giant perch. This full-bodied specimen weighed 5lb 9oz and is the fish that jointly holds the British record at a weight of 6lb 3oz.

MONSTERS!

Although commercial venues are often stuffed full of smaller fish, relative to the average size for species, they can also throw up some surprises. Commercials are now renowned for producing some monster perch to over 5lb, which grow big when left to thrive in an environment with an abundance of food and little or no competition from other predators! This is in stark contrast to rivers, because while they do hold outsize perch, many are shadows of their former selves, following predation by cormorants and otters. It may be that commercials come to dominate big-perch fishing in the future, and fish like Jim Mathews' giant become the norm at the top of the big-fish lists. Great tactics for commercial-water perching include float fishing in the margins and fishing with resistance-free running lead setups. Wily old perch can drop baits that are clumsily presented, especially when they feel resistance from the rod end. Big baits like cooked prawns as well as traditional combinations like lobworms and casters will work superbly for these stillwater predators, even in the quite coloured water that characterises most commercials. The scent trails that these baits give off will draw perch to them, even if they can't see them.

CHAPTER 5 CATCH CRAFTY CRUCIANS

Margin fishing with a float is as exciting as it gets! The action unfolds practically under your feet, with each pinprick bubble and knock of the float registering like a jolt to the nervous system! Although carp, tench, roach, rudd and perch can be caught close in, there is one species that is synonymous with the marginal shelf, and that's the buttery-yellow crucian carp.

The golden crucian is one of the UK's most beautiful species of fish.

Like the BFO lads, you'll find crucians close to marginal cover such as lily pads and reeds.

This shy-biting fish is one of the UK's most beautiful and elusive species. Unlike its bigger cousin the king carp, which was imported from Europe, the crucian is a true native of the British Isles. For many anglers it's a fish of the summer months, lily-studded pools and quiet farm ponds. Luckily for the BFO team, they knew just the place to find crucians… and big ones at that! Finding them can be tricky, but catching crucians can sometimes be harder still!

Dean shows Bobby the tackle they'll be using to target crucians. The pole is king and allows accurate presentation.

These hearty fighters demand a stealthy approach because they are often to be found hiding in cover such as lilies or reed beds, just inches from the bank. This makes the pole the ultimate tool for crucian fishing, because it allows the angler to present the finest, most sensitive tackle with pinpoint accuracy, right up against marginal cover.

Elasticated poles are perfect for battling feisty crucians, because they are robust fighters and often need to be steered away from snags. Although not the biggest fish in most waters, crucians fight hard, pound-for-pound, and the shock-absorbing elastic is key to landing them safely. On many waters, crucians share their home with fellow bottom-feeding species, tench and carp, so you can enjoy catching a mixed bag of fish, all from practically under your feet on the tactics described in this chapter.

The BFO visited the Bury Hill complex for this episode, a chain of lakes set in a wooded Surrey valley.

All of the lakes contained crucians, with some of them topping 3lb – true giants. First of all, the guests had to get to grips with the techniques that Dean and Ali had in mind. Setting up on Milton Lake, the teams quickly identified perfect crucian territory; shallow water shaded by large beds of lily pads and fringed by beds of flag iris. Although they can be tempted from open water, especially at dawn or dusk, the classic crucian swim has cover of some kind, be that lilies, reed beds, thick subsurface weed or overhanging trees and bushes. These compact bottom feeders seem to feel most at home with a roof over their heads during the day and can often be persuaded to feed close by. Before they could catch crucians though, the teams would have to get them feeding.

Traditional baits like sweetcorn and hempseed are a good starting point.

BAITING AND BAIT CHOICE

Crucians are suckers for a real variety of baits. These range from more traditional offerings like casters, maggots, redworms, bread and sweetcorn, through to thoroughly modern baits like pellets and mini boilies. They also show a real liking for groundbait and it is often the best way to spike their interest in the first instance.

As with all cyprinids, the crucian has a well-developed array of olfactory cells in the nares (nasal cavity) and on the head itself. These cells allow the detection of food signals very effectively indeed. As such, soluble liquid additives can be well worth adding to your groundbait. At Bury Hill, Ali and Ricky Groves used powerful-smelling King Crab Goo to glaze their pellet freebies, adding that all-important boost to the soluble attractors in the swim.

Although pellets possess a strong fishy aroma of their own, the addition of an attractive glaze certainly added to their effectiveness.

Ali and Ricky Groves opted to feed maggots and pellets as well.

TOP-FIVE CRUCIAN WATERS:

Marsh Farm
Hill Pond, Marsh Farm Fishery, Station Lane, Milford Surrey, GU8 5AE.
Perhaps the best crucian complex in the UK.
01483 428885
godalming.angling@gmail.com
www.godalminganglingsociety.co.uk

Milton Lake
Bury Hill Fishery, Westcott, nr Dorking, RH4 3JU.
As seen on The Big Fish Off!
Accesible fishing for good-sized crucians.
01245 325289
info@buryhillfisheries.com
www.buryhillfisheries.co.uk

Charity Farm Fishery
Smithy Brow, Toogood Lane, Wrightington, Nr Wigan, Lancashire, WN6 9PP.
Four landscaped pools set on a working farm.
01257 451326
www.charityfarm.co.uk

Soham Bypass Pit
Soham, Ely, Cambridgeshire
A four-acre lake next to the A142 near Soham with crucians to 3lb+
07877 165898
www.spotfish.co.uk/fishery/soham-by-pass-lake

Kingfisher Coarse Lake
Four Ponds Fishery, Shillingford, Devon, EX16 9BU
Day-ticket lake with crucians to 3lb
01398 331169
www.fourpondsfishery.com

Boosted pellets and groundbait are great fish-pullers, and will help you kick your swim off. Introduce them in small amounts for best results.

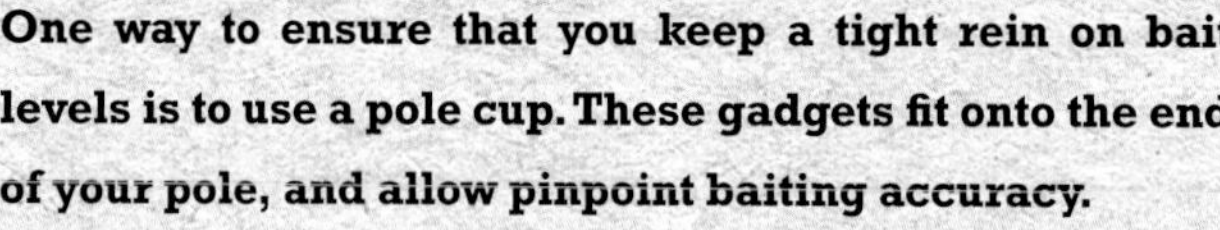

One way to ensure that you keep a tight rein on bait levels is to use a pole cup. These gadgets fit onto the end of your pole, and allow pinpoint baiting accuracy.

If, like Team Hamidi/Groves, you are going to include pellets in your bait armoury, a blend of smaller diameter versions is best. These can be dampened to increase the speed at which the attractors leak out into the water and the softening allows them to be hooked on easily. Ali and Ricky mixed their pellets with more the traditional loose-feed baits, sweetcorn, maggots and hemp. By introducing several types of bait, you can change your hook baits to find the one that the fish want on the day.

Crucians often feed in short bursts, fizzing up over your bait, before disappearing back into the cover of the lily pads, so try not to overload your swim. Keeping control of the amount of bait out there will allow you to maximise your chances of catching when the fish turn up for a feed.

Dean and Bobby Davro look suitably delighted with their bar of gold!

A bed of lilies on Bury Hill's Milton Lake produced a run of crucians for Ali and Ricky.

TACKLING UP

Crucian fishing is mostly carried out close to the bank, so it's rare that you'll need to use a pole of more than 10m. Because you may well encounter bigger species, such as tench and carp when targeting this kind of marginal habitat, a longer, put-together pole is recommended, rather than a short whip pole. If you have a long float rod, 13ft or 14ft, then this can also make an excellent choice, especially when fishing at ultra-close range. Couple it with a centrepin loaded with 3lb line and you have a versatile setup that can be used to drop a pole float tight to marginal pads, yet is capable of subduing bigger quarry, should you hook them.

Whether you're using a pole or a float rod, your rigs will be very similar.

Hitting the subtle bites is key in crucian fishing, so a sensitive bristle pole float is vital.

These floats can be shotted right down, so that the slightest tap is visible. Because of the way they feed, sucking up baits while standing on their heads, crucians can be very hard to hook, so be prepared to miss more bites than you hook!

Often, as crucians feed around your hook bait, the float will sway and dance – these indications are called 'liners', caused as the fish rub up against your line, and should not be struck at. Wait for a definite bob or lift before striking. Using the correct shotting pattern will help you identify more crucian bites. The most crucial shot is the one nearest your hook. This 'telltale' shot, so called because it gives the game away for the biting fish, should be positioned within a couple of inches of the hook. This way, if a fish sucks the bait in and lifts away from the lake bed, the bite will register as a slight lift on the float.

To make the most of this sensitive rig, you should set the float so that the hook bait lies on the lake bed. Crucians will be searching for their food on the bottom, so this is where your hook bait should be!

This is easily achieved with the use of a plummet; simply move the float up and down the line until it sits out on your chosen spot as it would when cocked properly. Then, simply slide it up the line an inch or so, which will ensure that the hook bait is presented right where you want it, among your free bait.

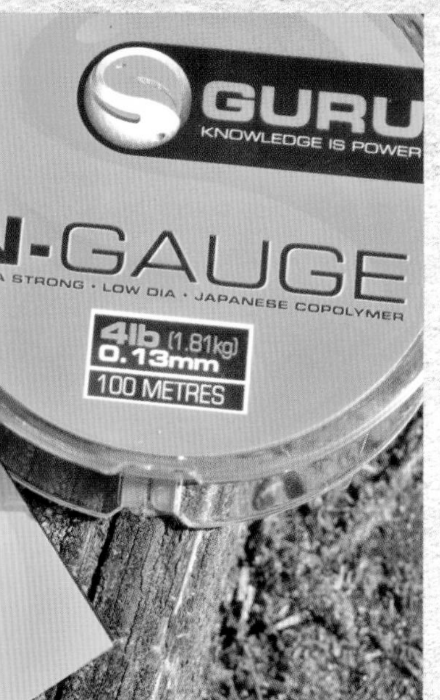

Ali set up an elasticated pole with a bristle-type pole float and size-18 hooks, perfect crucian tackle.

Treat your quarry with the utmost care, however kissing is optional!

The proximity of tough snags such as lilies demands that robust tackle is used for margin fishing. If you find crucians feeding in an open-water swim, then you can scale back your tackle accordingly. Assuming you're fishing close to snags, we'd recommend a main line of at least 3lb, and a hook link of 2.5lb. A forged hook pattern in the size range 18 to 14 is perfect. Ali and Ricky opted for the Guru MWG pattern in size 18 for their Milton Lake session. These super-strong hooks are perfect for a range of baits and are beefy enough to steer crucian, tench or carp away from danger.

Crucian fishing can be among the most frustrating, yet ultimately rewarding experiences in our sport. When they're obliging, you can quickly fill your net with gold, but when they're being coy, you'll have to work extra hard for a single specimen!

They're a great test of angling ability and tactical nous and, big or small, are one of our most beautiful species.

A softened pellet hook bait is perfect crucian fodder and matches a size-18 hook nicely.

DID YOU KNOW?

Crucians (Carassius carrasius) are notoriously difficult to identify, thanks to the fact that they readily hybridise (interbreed) with king carp (Cyprinius carpio) or the brown goldfish (Carassius auratus). There are, however a few simple ways to tell if you've caught a true cru'! Firstly, true crucians have no barbules at all! If your capture has stumpy barbules – it's not a crucian. Counting the scales that run along the lateral line (the sensory organ that runs along the middle of a fishes' flank, seen as a broken line) is another good test. If you can count 32 to 34 scales, you've most likely got a true crucian. Taken in isolation, neither of these tests is conclusive, so it's worth checking the fins of your catch too. The dorsal fin should be convex, and the tail (or caudal) fin should be straight, or only slightly forked, when extended vertically.

Several fisheries pride themselves in having verified crucians and the National Crucian Conservation Project was set up in 2014 to preserve the true crucian, in the face of increasing hybridisation.

There simply can't be a prettier fish to target, can there? They're tricky to outwit too, so provide a challenge.

ALTERNATIVE TACTICS

Those fishing for the very biggest crucians have moved away from traditional methods, towards a style of fishing that has more in common with carp fishing. Specimen hunters pioneered the use of self-hooking bolt rigs for crucian fishing. This is largely due to the difficult nature of the fishing on larger venues.

Being able to fish multiple rods on bite alarms certainly helps to stack the odds in the favour of the angler who's seeking the very biggest crucians on lakes that contain a handful of giants. Inline leads or method feeders, coupled with short braided hook links and hair rigs are now the order of the day on crucian super-waters!

It is likely that this style of fishing will continue to dominate the crucian big-fish lists for the foreseeable future.

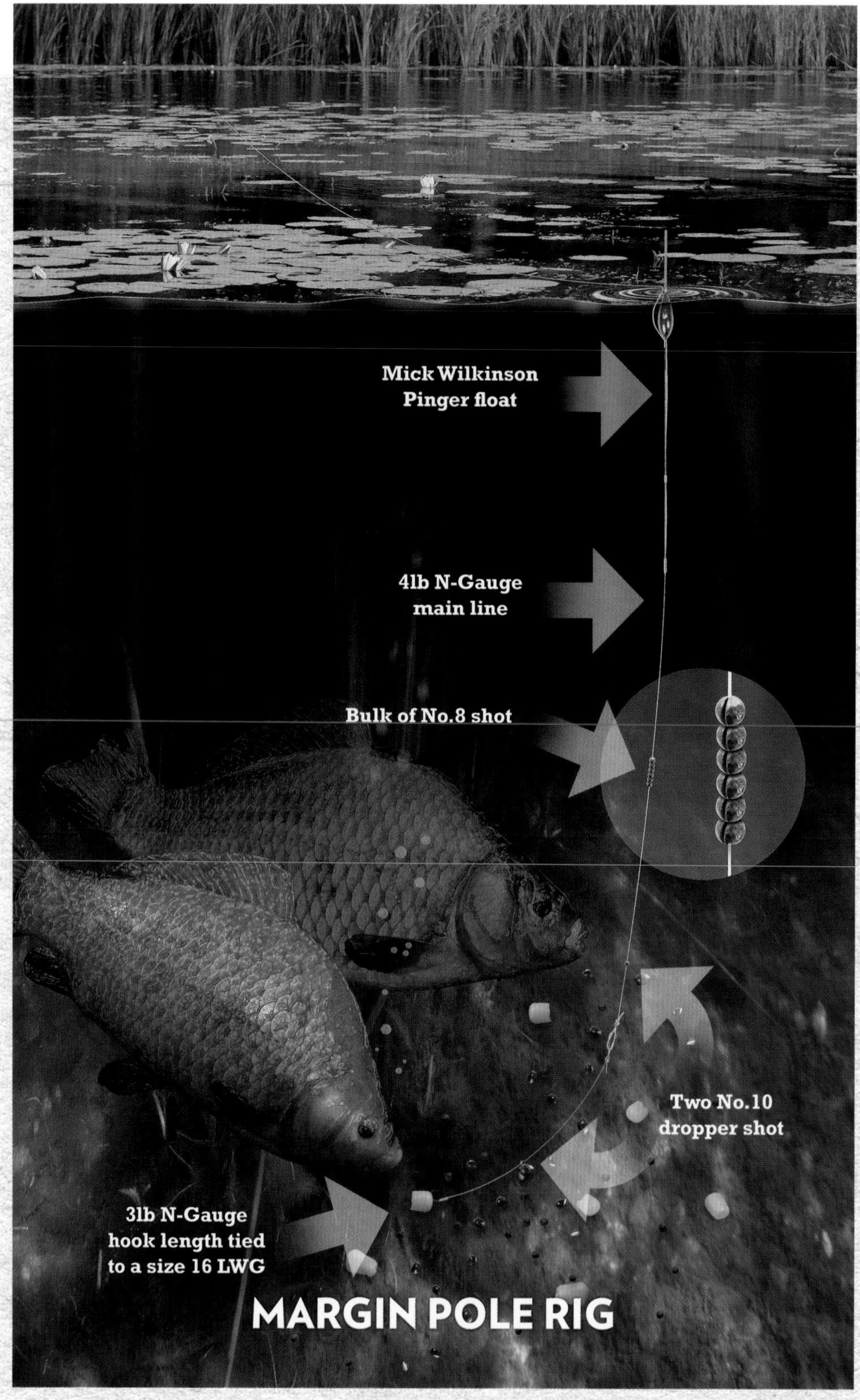

Mick Wilkinson
Pinger float

4lb N-Gauge
main line

Bulk of No.8 shot

Two No.10
dropper shot

3lb N-Gauge
hook length tied
to a size 16 LWG

MARGIN POLE RIG

With Ali out for revenge, he was keen to bank as many of these as possible!

BEHIND THE SCENES

This wasn't the first time the Big Fish Off had pitted the teams in a quest for crucians. Those of you who watched season one of the show will surely remember 'Cruciangate', as it became known! Tasked with catching crucians in deepest Norfolk, Ali and old school friend, the cricketer Graham Napier, thought they'd pipped Dean and Eastenders actor, Scott Maslen, by banking the only crucian of the show. However, with other species counting towards the final totals, team Macey notched a controversial victory, despite not landing a single crucian! Ali was left fuming, and was after revenge when the BFO cameras rolled at Bury Hill with crucians once again the target!

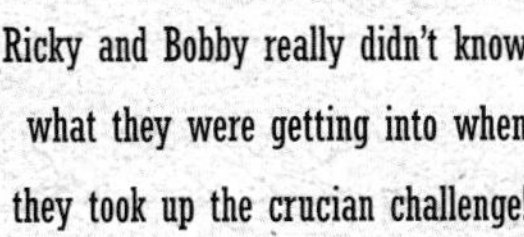

Ricky and Bobby really didn't know what they were getting into when they took up the crucian challenge!

MONSTER CRUCIANS!
DEAN MACEY

I was about 12 years old when I set eyes on a crucian carp for the very first time. Unfortunately, it was during a fishing match that I wasn't doing that well in. So, at about half time I decided to go a wander around the lake to see how everyone else was doing. Just as I approached an angler sitting on his DIY fishing box, he landed the most amazing buttery-coloured carp I had ever seen. I was too shy to ask what it was but as it slid back into the lily-covered margins, I knew I had to catch one for myself. Little did I know that this was to become an almost impossible dream for so long, due to the lack of crucians in the lakes I was fishing and my VERY bullish approach to catching them.

Over the years, as my methods and knowledge grew, so did my success with the species, culminating in catching my first three pounder. And believe you me, when they get to that size they really do look something else! Not happy with that, I set about upping my personal best almost every year by an ounce or two.

One sunny summer afternoon while filming a Fishing Gurus show for Sky Sports, we decided to target crucians on a venue that had a reputation for throwing up the odd big fish. Well, while bugging some bubblers in a quiet little corner of the lake, one of my rods signalled a take. I was on it in a flash and at first thought it was a reasonable tench. As it rolled on the surface I couldn't believe my eyes; it was a massive crucian. All the presenting went out the window, all I wanted was to get this creature into the net as soon as possible.

Dean's huge crucian fell to his rods while filming for Fishing Gurus. At 3lb 11oz, it was a true monster.

It's fair to say I got myself into a little bit of a flap! I kid you not, when we weighed her at 3lb 11oz I went a little funny in the head.

It was the biggest crucian I had ever seen, and it was mine to hold up to the cameras. Moments like that are why we go fishing!

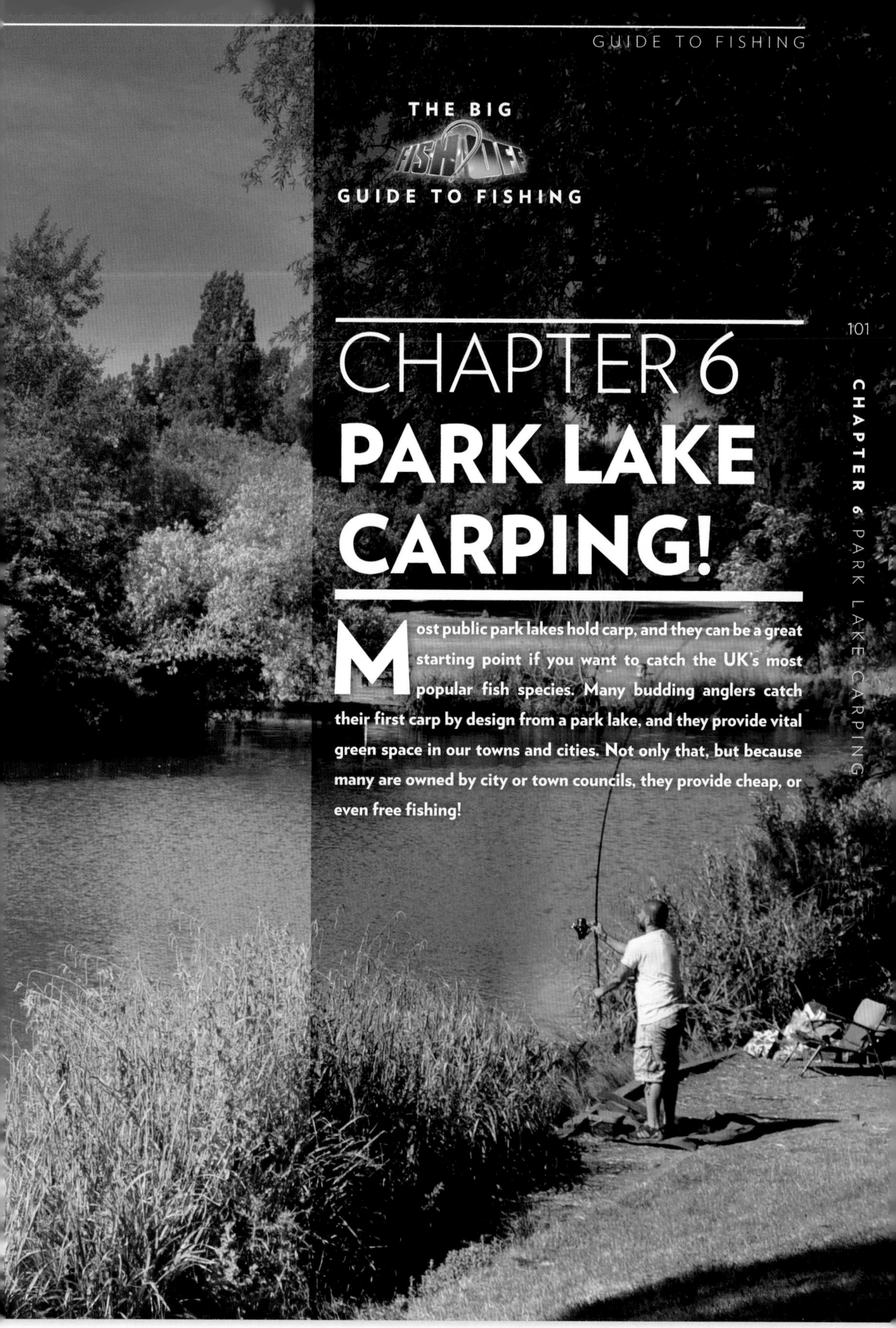

THE BIG FISH'N'LIFE GUIDE TO FISHING

CHAPTER 6 PARK LAKE CARPING!

Most public park lakes hold carp, and they can be a great starting point if you want to catch the UK's most popular fish species. Many budding anglers catch their first carp by design from a park lake, and they provide vital green space in our towns and cities. Not only that, but because many are owned by city or town councils, they provide cheap, or even free fishing!

Park lakes can be found in most larger cities and towns – and many hold a good stock of hard-fighting carp, like the one being weighed by Dean and Sally.

Dean and Sally see exactly how big her first park-lake carp is!

You're unlikely to find an oasis of calm amid the urban sprawl, but the rewards that lurk below the water's surface make up for the lack of seclusion. For The Big Fish Off Episode 4 Ali and Dean took their teammates, Anna Kelle and Sally Gunnell, to Gloucester Park in Basildon. The park has special appeal for Dean, as it's where he spent many hours chasing carp as a teenager. The question was, would the carp be as obliging a decade or two later?

The teams pitched up opposite a long, tree-lined island that was a known haunt for the carp and the fish soon announced their presence. If you fancy a crack at park carping then the good news is that the fish can often be found relatively easily! Let's take a look at the kind of features that are common to park lakes...

A pungent bait cast close to an island was a recipe for succcess on the Essex park lake for Ali and AK.

Many park lakes have islands that were scuplted for aesthetic reasons, but also provide great nesting sites for birds, and refuge for fish. Because so many park lakes also have uniform, concrete banks, and flat, weedless lake beds, the islands, their overhanging trees and undercut banks, are the most significant features on the whole lake. It's often a good starting point to cast your bait as close to the island as you can manage, because carp patrol the island margins, looking for food all year round. You'd be surprised at just how undercut those margins can be too, making them all the more attractive to carp. Quite often, a bait cast right under the overhangs will produce action within minutes, rather than hours on the more prolific waters. the difference between getting a bite and not can be as little as a few inches when it comes to casting to islands, so it pays to get it right!

Because of their age, many park lakes tend to be dammed streams, rather than the gravel pits and purpose-dug fisheries that make up a large proportion of more recently created venues. This means that there will often be an inflow, definite shallows, a deeper dam end and an outflow. Because the inflow deposits sediment, the shallows into which it flows will often have a soft, silty (fine particles of decaying organic matter) bottom. Carp love to 'truffle' around in this soft stuff, picking out areas that are rich in bloodworm to focus their attention. You can often find fish quite easily when they're feeding in the shallower water, thanks to the mud clouds that they stir up.

A stealthy approach is needed to ensure that the fish don't spook when you cast out though. Repeated casting is one way to ensure that the fish leave the area!

DID YOU KNOW?

Dean Macey was on familiar territory for this challenge, because he used to fish at Gloucester Park when he was a student in the area. Many of the carp that Dean used to fish for are still alive, meaning that the Gloucester Park carp are really rather old.

The oldest recorded carp in UK carp history lived in Redmire Pool, a famous lake in Herefordshire. The fish, Raspberry, was stocked in 1934 and lived to the grand old age of 67! Redmire occupies a special place in the history of carp fishing, having produced a string of record carp between the 1950s and 1981.

TOP TIP

Ali soaks his Mainline Peaches & Cream wafters in Mangonana Supreme Goo.

By loading his Infuza (a special bait tub, designed for soaking hook baits) with the wafters, and a good squirt of the Goo, he's able to create a super-attractive hook bait that will attract carp, and repel the smell of silt. Many park lakes are extremely silty and the decaying organic matter will overpower weaker-smelling baits. You'll see that the thin Supreme Goo cuts into the skin of the bait, allowing it to produce a mouth-watering scent trail the whole time your baits are in the water.

Because the Infuza has a removable slotted tray, in which the baits sit, they won't become over-glugged in the Goo, which sits in a well beneath the tray. To re-glug the baits, simply shake the tub, which coats the baits and the Goo can drain away to the base again. The result… perfectly soaked wafters!

The more times you repeat the process, the further the Goo will soak into the bait and the longer it will pump out attractors. Ali has pots of Goo'd hook baits that he's had soaking for years!

Perfectly prepared wafters, ready to snare a park lake carp.

Most park lakes hold a range of fish species, so fishing with boilies is the best way to ensure that your bait finds the intended species. Dean Macey loves to use 10mm boilies at Gloucester Park, spraying them out with a catapult, but if you have a large stock of tench, bream or roach, then you may want to consider using boilies of 15mm or 18mm in size. Boilies represent the ultimate in convenience and effectiveness. Both shelf-life boilies (preserved) and freezer (fresh) baits will work on parks, although shelf life baits tend to be a little tougher-skinned, making them a little more resistant to the attentions of birds, or smaller species. What's more, you can keep them between sessions without having to access to a freezer. It's always worth carrying a selection of pellets too, as they are attractive to every carp that swims. They can be combined with some crumbled boilies to make an attractive PVA bag mix. Squeeze a blob of Goo onto the outside of the mesh bag and you've got a concentrated parcel of attraction that will draw carp directly to your hook bait, no matter how stinky the silt is!

A blob of Goo on the outside of a PVA bag gives extra punch, when fishing in stinky silt.

Arriving before first light, if allowed, is the best way to make sure your location is spot on.

Many park lakes only allow fishing from dawn to dusk, so making the most of every minute is paramount. You can do this by ensuring that you arrive as soon as access is allowed, and take as little gear as you can. The more kit you carry, the less inclined you'll be to move around, which will cost you chances of locating the carp. Spotting carp within the first hour of being at the lake, especially if that's around dawn, is the biggest shortcut to success. A bait cast to fish that show during the early morning can often produce a quick bite.

If you have a barrow, then you can leave much of your kit loaded on top, ready to move if you spot fish.

If you can't spot any carp crashing out, clouding up the water or bubbling, then trying a new swim every hour is a good tactic. You can enhance your chances of success by baiting up in advance of your session too. It's a good idea to fish over a small number of free baits, so getting the carp accustomed to finding food in the spots that you plan to fish can help to cut the time you'll be waiting for a bite. Korda's Tom Dove uses this tactic to great effect at Walthamstow Reservoirs, which, apart from designated weekends, is a day-only complex. He heads up to his chosen reservoir and trickles a few hundred baits into a couple of swims the evening before he intends to fish. These pre-baiting tactics can yield quick results, because the fish are likely to be searching for more boilies in the area that's been pre-baited. When you arrive, introduce twenty or thirty baits at most over your hook baits to keep the fish searching out baits.

PARK LAKES TO TRY

Walton Hall Park, Liverpool
Free fishing for medium-sized carp in an urban setting.
www.liverpool.gov.uk/leisure-parks-and-events/angling/

Coate Water Park, Swindon
Big carp on a very famous night syndicate in the south west.
www.swindon.gov.uk

Broadwater Lake, Godalming
Extremely prolific carp lake with plenty of doubles and some crafty twenty pounders!
www.godalminganglingsociety.co.uk

Sutton Park, Birmingham
Blackroot and Powell's hold some good carp and have a special place in local carp history.
www.birmingham.gov.uk

Milton Country Park, Cambridge
Prolific carp fishing for double-figure carp in one of the UKs prettiest cities.
www.miltoncountrypark.org

A scattering of free offerings soon bought Dean and Sally some park lake action as they stormed into the lead.

Dean and Sally with a cracking Gloucester Park common. Who knows, perhaps one of the carp that Dean used to catch as a student?

When casting tight to islands it's wise to use a simple rig that resists tangles!

Ali chose to use a running rig on Gloucester Park, which is another effective setup. The lake bed was firm enough (determined by how defined the 'thud' of the lead hitting the bottom is when it transmits up the line), so he set up his lead system so that the lead could run freely on the line. This method can work especially well for park lake carp that have seen it all in terms of rigs. Because the lead isn't fixed like it would be with a conventional lead clip, the fish can't use the weight of the lead to throw the hook, which pressured carp can do! For ultimate convenience Ali coupled his running rig setup with a ready-tied Krank rig (see the rig diagram for more details on how Ali constructed his setup). He used a slow-sinking boilie hook bait, called a 'wafter'. These baits have been designed to mimic your freebies, and settle slowly on top of the lake bed. Because they're a little more buoyant, these wafters ensure that the hook bait acts more like a free bait when disturbed by carp feeding close by.

Without extra buoyancy, the weight of the hook and rig would make the bait noticeably heavier than the freebies!

SHOPPING LIST

- 12ft 2.75lb Daiwa Long-bow Carp Rods
- 5000 size free-spool reels
- 12lb Touchdown main line
- Lightweight 50-inch brolly
- Lightweight low chair
- Small rucksack
- Size-six Krank Ready Rigs
- Korda Lead Clip Action Pack
- 2.5oz Flat Pear Leads

A wafter hook bait acts naturally in the water with the weight of the hook just sinking the boilie. It'll fly into the mouth of a feeding carp if it sucks at the bait, though!

Dark Matter rig tubing

Size 6 Krank Ready Rig

Guru Micro Lead Clip sliding on the main line

ALI'S PARK LAKE RIG

Ali runs AK through the tackle needed for their park lake session.

Given that many park lakes are under twenty acres in size, there's no call for super-heavy casting gear, or big-pit reels. The one exception is if the lake is heavily weeded. In that situation, it pays to have a rod with extra power, to help extract a weeded fish so we'd suggest stepping up to 3.25lb or 3.5lb models. For the most part, however, carp rods of around 2.75lb test curve, and free-spool reels loaded with 12lb line are more than adequate for casting up to 100 yards if needed. The more forgiving action will allow you to enjoy the fight of a park lake carp when you hook one! Because public lakes often don't allow night fishing, you won't need to lug a full bivvy or bedchair around with you. A fifty-inch brolly and low chair will keep you sheltered and comfortable in all but the most tempestuous weather.

Oh, and don't forget the stove. Having access to hot drinks and food will keep your spirits and motivation up, meaning you'll still be there if the carp only begin to feed at the very end of the day!

For the price of a day ticket, park lake fishing often provides prolific action, in lively, landscaped surroundings. The carp are often from a mix of sources, and many parks hold old, sought-after specimens. If you're looking for a way into carp fishing, then park lakes will give you a solid grounding.

Park lake carping is a great way to get into fishing for larger fiish on heavier tackle.

THE BIG FISH OFF GUIDE TO FISHING

MONSTERS!

LUKE VALLORY

When I first walked around the big park lake, I remember being in awe at its size and surroundings; I knew then that I wasn't ready to take on the challenge. I was out of my comfort zone! I was accustomed to fishing much smaller waters, which were far more isolated from the general public, whereas the park lake has a pubic footpath access all the way around it. The stock of carp was also quite low per acre, which made me feel more doubtful of success, as I was used to fishing smaller lakes with more carp.

Even so, I was filled with excitement when beginning my new quest and was looking forward to the journey. The lake had so much to offer, even though it was slap-bang in the middle of a public park and had a railway line adjacent to it. It still had that sense of wildness, due to its many features and unique shape. The lake had so much character and offered different styles of fishing, you could be tucked away in one of the many overgrown bays, fishing to big islands, or out in the open water up against the elements when Mother Nature springs up a big wind, with white waves crashing in front of you!

The park lake really did get under my skin, it always kept me on my toes and I had to endure the hard times when things weren't going so well. However, that only made me want it more and, ultimately, I became more motivated to achieve my dreams.

Luke's park lake monsters; a 35lb mirror (top right) and a 37-pounder (bottom), caught by fishing short sessions and moving regularly when he saw fish showing.

The thrill of the chase meant that I had to keep going until I was rewarded for my efforts. The feeling when you're cradling a big carp, after working hard for that capture, is so special! Follow your dreams and aspirations because the rewards can be great!

Fishing from a boat offers a different set of challenges - but it can be lots of fun and a productive way of fishing otherwise inaccessible areas.

CHAPTER 7 GOING AFLOAT

There's little better than spending a summer's day afloat on a serene English estate lake, watching the bright tip of a waggler riding the gentle ripple. Although there are relatively few lakes that allow fishing from punts, waggler tactics are useful for targeting most waters that hold fish like tench, bream, perch and roach from the bank as well. One lake that does offer punts to fish from though, is Old Bury Hill, the setting for challenge two of show one, which pitted Ali Hamidi and Ricky Groves against Dean Macey and Bobby Davro.

FIVE TO TRY

Old Bury Hill, Surrey
Hire punts from the boathouse and set sail out onto this stunning Surrey estate lake. Tench and bream are the targets.
www.buryhillfishery.co.uk

Blenheim Palace, Oxon
Fish for tench and bream from a boat on the stunning lake at Winston Churchill's birthplace in Oxfordshire.
www.blenheimpalace.com

The Trinity Broads, Norfolk
Try Ormesby, Rollesby and Filby Broads for roach, bream and tench
www.broads-authority.gov.uk

Tabley Mere, Knutsford
Beautiful club water that allows fishing from boats for carp, tench and bream.
www.lymmanglersclub.com

Hanningfield Reservoir, Essex
Any-method trout fishing from a boat, which is great fun for youngsters and families. Run by Essex & Suffolk Water. Cafe and full facilites on site.
www.eswater.co.uk

The boat house at Old Bury Hill - a great venue to try fishing afloat for this first time.

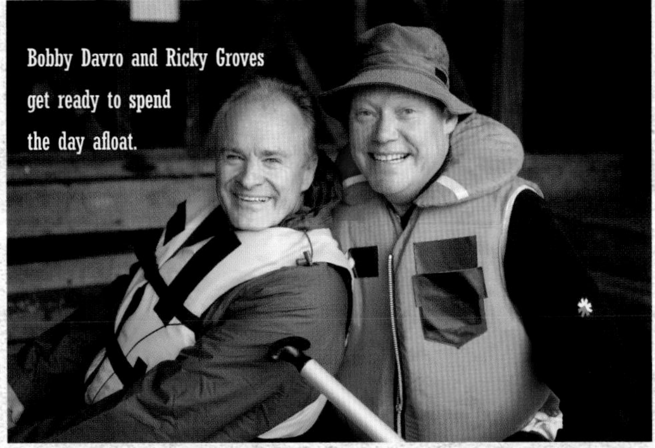
Bobby Davro and Ricky Groves get ready to spend the day afloat.

Both teams took care to wear the correct safety equipment, including suitable life jackets.

The sun was high in a flawless blue sky when the teams set off across the ancient estate lake (they'd had a hearty breakfast first!)... hardly the perfect conditions for bream, their target species. Both tench and bream are fish of the twilight, preferring to feed around dawn or dusk. So, unlike our sparring teams, we'd suggest that you head to your lake as early as possible, if you want to target tench and bream most effectively! Fishing a running line, as opposed to a pole, allows you to fish much further out into the lake, which is a bonus if bream are the target.

Let's take a look at why that is, by discussing open-water fishing with the waggler...

A good quality mono main line will allow you to cast well out into the lake, where the larger fish patrol.

Because it's fished with a rod and reel, the waggler can be cast well out into the lake, where shoals of slab-sided bream patrol. Bream are predominately a fish of the open water, and they can be highly nomadic, moving between feeding areas along regular routes, often clipping the surface as they do. This behaviour, known as porpoising, is a dead giveaway that bream are on the move, and you can often tell in which direction they are traveling! Fishing the waggler allows you to get out onto these patrol routes, and a bed of bait will often stop bream in their tracks, allowing you to cash in until they move on again.

A float rod of at least 13ft and small, match-sized reel is perfect for waggler fishing.

We'd recommend a fast-taper float rod (one which has a stiff butt and middle, with a forgiving tip), which will allow you to punch a bait up to 30 yards out into the lake. It's absolutely vital that you fill your reel with high performance line for waggler fishing, partly because a quality line will be much more supple and whisper through the rod rings, imparting much less drag on the float, and partly because it's likely to be thinner for its breaking strain, allowing longer casts to be made. Guru Pulse Line in 4lb is ideal for waggler fishing, because it's supple, thin and strong. Because they're fixed at the bottom end, wagglers allow you to sink the line from the tip of the rod, to the float itself. This is critical

With both teams fishing towards the far-bank features, accurate casting and keeping the link sunk was essential to present the hook bait properly.

when there's wind, and good practice even when there isn't, because it helps the float stay right where you need it, over your bait! To sink the line, simply cast the float a few yards beyond the area that you're fishing, dip the rod tip and make several quick turns of the reel. When the float pops up over your spot, the line will have cut through the surface film. The further out you're fishing, the further you'll have to overcast to get your line sunk. Remember, dipping the tip further, and reeling faster will sink your line more effectively!

Macey and Davro take the lead in the boat battle, do you think Dean's happy about it?

DID YOU KNOW?

Many fish are what is known as crepuscular, meaning that they are most active at dawn or dusk – the transitional periods between day and night. Tench, bream and carp all feed at night too, but first light is often the best time to catch them. Fish exhibit this pattern of behaviour because they're either avoiding being eaten, or searching for food themselves. Lakes and rivers can be extremely active at dawn and dusk because fish are either moving to shelter, or coming out to feed. Watching carefully at this time will allow you to locate groups of feeding fish, which is essential!

If you can spot fish breaking the surface, then you can save yourself a lot of time spent in the wrong area. As the old adage goes, it's better to spend five minutes in the right spot than hours in the wrong spot. A pair of binoculars can prove a worthwhile addition to your kit to watch for rolling bream. Once located, the fish may tolerate you casting into the area, but if they don't it's best to bait the area and head back the next morning, lay your traps and wait their return.

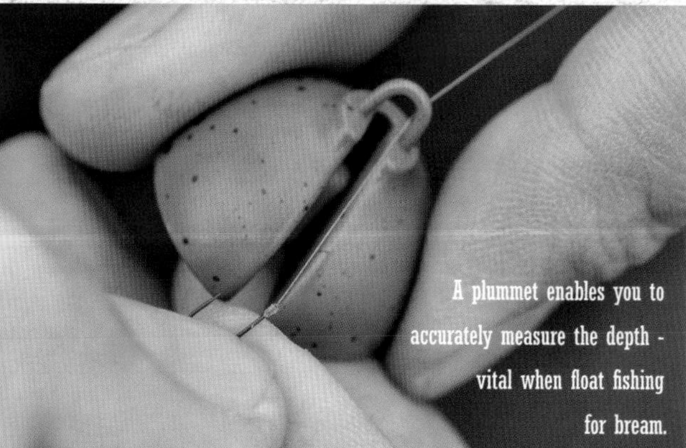

A plummet enables you to accurately measure the depth - vital when float fishing for bream.

WHERE TO CAST!

Your first priority should be to watch for porpoising or rolling bream on the surface, but if you can't see them, then here are our tips for finding those bream feeding areas! Bream prefer deep water and they love to move along subsurface features like gravel bars, old riverbeds or shelves. It's almost like they choose to navigate along these aquatic roadways! Targeting the rear slope of a gravel bar, or the deepest point of an old streambed (usually found in dammed estate lakes), is a good way to start and can often put you right onto the bream superhighway! If you can find a ledge where the marginal shelf drops off into deeper water, then that's also a great starting point, whether you're on an intimate pond, or a vast Irish lough. Finding these areas can take careful plumbing of the depths. There are two ways that you can do this. Firstly, you can attach a plummet to your float setup and cast around, adjusting the float to measure the depths in each part of the swim. Secondly, you can strip your float off the line, tie a 1oz bomb onto the end and cast it around the swim, counting how long it takes to hit the bottom. Allowing roughly 1 second per foot of depth will give you a good idea of the topography of the swim. It's best to do this when you're not actually fishing – perhaps the night before, so you don't disturb the area too much.

If you are heading to the lake before fishing, it's often a good idea to prebait your swim, once you've found the spot that you plan to fish. Which takes us nicely onto baiting!

Pellets are a great bream bait - they love the fishy taste and smell given off as they break down in the water.

WHICH BAIT?

Luckily, bream and tench love baits that are cheap and widely available. Traditionally, cereal-based groundbaits, breadcrumb, sweetcorn, trout pellets and hempseed have been relied upon to draw fish into your swim, and hold them there. Of course, maggots and especially casters have their place alongside these cheaper baits and worms hold a special appeal for bream. To really increase your chances, take a selection of hook bait options and use them in combination. These hook baits are called cocktails, and combos such as worm and caster, worm and sweetcorn, and caster and sweetcorn are proven winners.

To start with, you should always look to put down a bed of bait that will stop bream in their tracks.

Usually, given the ranges involved, that means using groundbait and a groundbait catapult. The base for your groundbait can be made from breadcrumbs, commercially available groundbaits, or even maize-based dog foods like Vitalin, all of which will bind well and hold plenty of your hook bait samples, allowing you to get these lighter items out into the swim, beyond the range that you'd usually be able to catapult them. To help form the groundbait balls, you need to dampen

Casters (top), hemp and sweetcorn (middle) and groundbait laced with maggots (bottom) are also great baits.

Chopped worm is a favourite bait to draw bream to your swim - the juices released by cutting up a handful of lobworms are irresistable.

the mix. This is usually done with lake water, but you can add liquid attractants at this stage too, which will get a scent trail out into your swim as soon as the groundbait hits the lake bed! Traditional liquid food winners worth trying include corn steep liquor (a by-product of corn milling) and liquid molasses (a sweet, sticky by-product of sugar refining), or you could go ultra-modern with watered-down Corn Twist Goo from Kiana carp, a fish magnet!

By mixing in sweetcorn, casters, maggots, hempseed, and chopped worms, you can give the fish a real buffet to choose from, allowing you to rotate your cocktail hook baits until you find the one the fish want on the day. A dozen balls of groundbait will create a carpet of food that's attractive enough to stop a shoal of bream for long enough to catch a few! Bream can be extremely flighty fish, so topping up with groundbait balls while they're still in the area could drive them away, so wait until there has been a real lull in the action before you top up!

Modern specimen hunters often use mini-boilies for bream now, along with fake casters and maggots. These baits allow the angler to be confident that his/her hook baits are still on, many hours after you cast them out. This is key when you're fishing for wily old bream that may only come in to feed once during your session.

END TACKLE

We'd recommend carrying a selection of wagglers, to account for all conditions, including peacock and insert crystal wagglers. Many insert wagglers allow you to change from an orange or yellow tip, to a black tip so you can see the float well in all light conditions. In very bright conditions, with lots of reflected light, it can be much better to use a black-tipped float. On duller days, the traditional orange or yellow tends to be a better bet!

You can black-off the tips of a few of your peacock wagglers with a permanent marker too, which will have the same effect.

Because you're going to need to cast a fair way, carrying some big wagglers, which take up to 4SSG shot to cock them is essential. For close-in fishing, more delicate insert wagglers are perfect (around the 3BB size). By grouping the shot just above your hook link, as shown in the diagram, you can ensure that the bait travels quickly through the water column and won't be snatched by smaller species, which live in the upper layers. Generally, you should set your float to lay at least a couple of inches of line on the bottom for bream and tench fishing. The windier it is, the more line you may have to fish overdepth to hold position in your swim.

Having a number of pre-tied hook links is always a good idea. Because the feeding window for bream may only be for the first hour or two of the day, time is of the essence and being prepared will mean you spend more time fishing and less time retackling! A hook link of around 2.5lb, tied to hooks ranging from 18 up to 14 will be perfect and will allow you to use baits as small as a single caster, right up to larger worm cocktails.

BEHIND THE SCENES

The difference between what is broadcast and the reality while filming can be stark! It might have looked serene on TV, but filming this challenge for the BFO was far from it! Rather than simply the two punts that you see on screen, there were actually five used, four of which were lashed together to form a floating set that housed two cameramen, a director, a photographer the two teams and enough food and drink to keep everyone fed and watered for a day afloat! It's surprisingly difficult to stay quiet when you've got a whole production team moored up in the shallows! Despite this, the bream and tench still fed, so imagine what you can do if you're actually able to take a stealthy approach! Not that we're making excuses or anything...

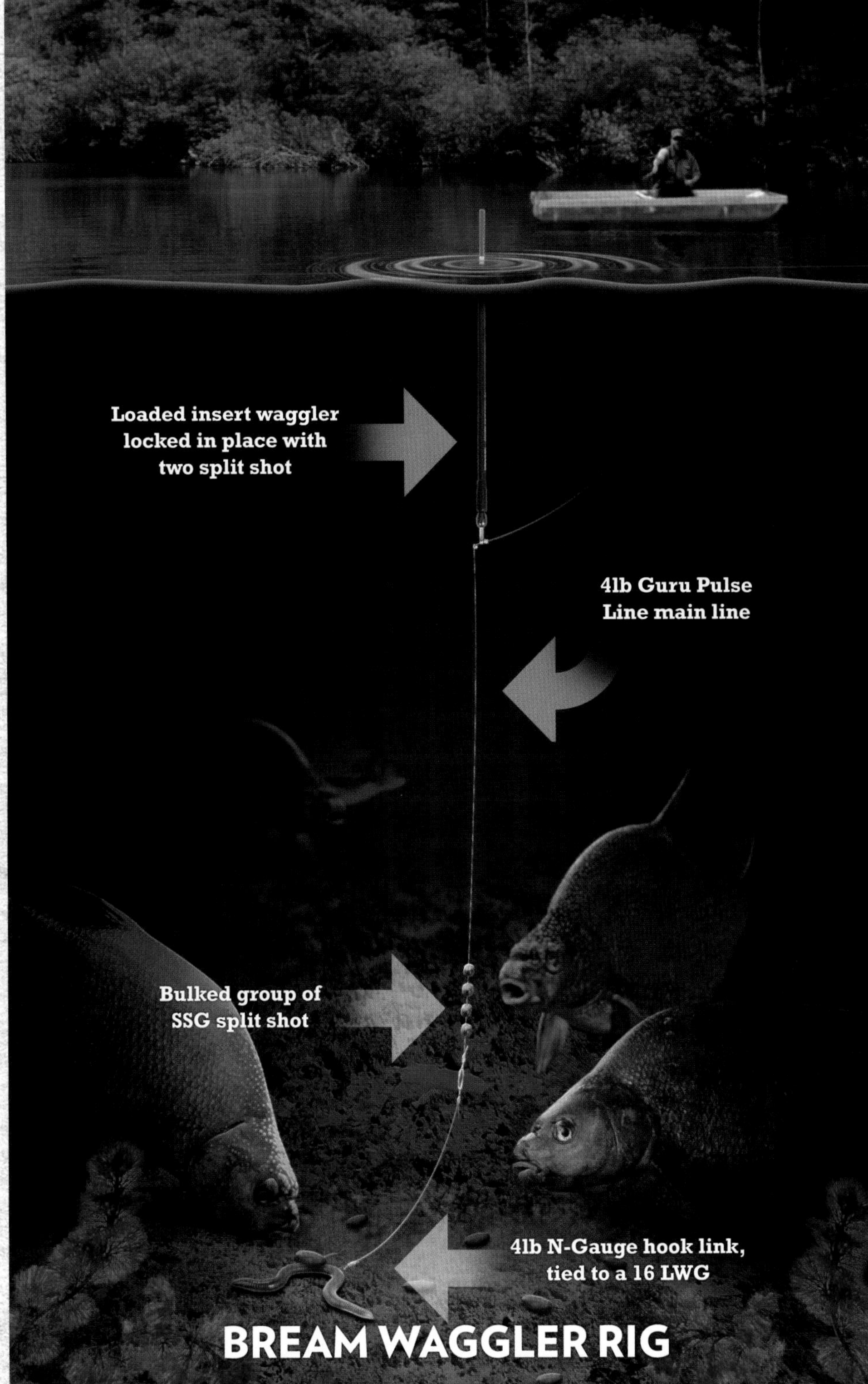
Loaded insert waggler locked in place with two split shot
4lb Guru Pulse Line main line
Bulked group of SSG split shot
4lb N-Gauge hook link, tied to a 16 LWG
BREAM WAGGLER RIG

Ricky Groves plays a bream to the net in front of The Big Fish Off cameras.

Although we've discussed waggler fishing in open water until now, there is no reason that a less weighty setup can't be used close in, where tench lurk close to weed and snags. In fact, by simply attaching a smaller float, you can use the waggler setup much as you would a pole, to fish close to pads, reeds or snaggy bushes for tench and smaller carp. The baits are the same, the rigs are the same, but you're more likely to encounter these other cyprinid species close in. Using a running line gives you more chance of stopping a hard-fighting carp or tench too! To take your game to the next level, try raking your margin swim with a weighty garden rake head tied to some rope! The rake will disturb the lake bed and kick up invertebrates like freshwater shrimps, hoglouse and bloodworms, the natural food of fish. You'll be amazed at how quickly the fish will move in to feed, despite the disturbance!

As you can see, the waggler is a versatile weapon, which can be deployed in open water or close to snags, in high winds, or on mill-pond-calm mornings.

Once you see those bubbles peppering the surface, close to your float, the adrenaline will kick in and you'll be hooked forever!

GOING AFLOAT

If you're lucky enough to spend the day afloat, then there are some key things you need to consider. First, and most importantly – wear a lifejacket. No ifs, no buts, this is the single most important piece of advice that you'll ever take. After that, make sure that somebody knows that you're heading out, and let them know when you plan to be back.

Once you're out in the boat, you need to be self-sufficient, so make sure that you take plenty of fluids and food! A cool-box can be a good addition to the kit if the day is hot; you'll lose concentration quickly if you're hungry or thirsty. Finally, make sure you pack some sun cream and a wide-brimmed hat! There's no shade out in the middle of the lake, so stay safe if you're out all day.

Once out in the boat, you need to be able to anchor up within comfortable casting distance of the swim. Usually, boats or punts are supplied with mudweights on chains, which are deployed at each end of the boat to hold it in place. You can make your own by filling a bucket with concrete and setting a metal loop into the base of it to attach a rope to! Cheap and effective!

Ali and Ricky with a typical float-caught Old Bury Hill bream.

THE BIG FISH OFF GUIDE TO FISHING

MONSTERS!
DEAN MACEY

Bream are not the prettiest or hardest fighting fish you'll ever catch but as it was the first ever fish I caught when I was 12 years old, I will always have a soft spot for them! Back then I was fishing for bream of 2-3lb, now however, with a little more knowledge and experience, I find myself targeting them to well over 10lb. And no matter what Ali says, a double-figure bream is quite an impressive looking creature.

Over the last few years I've had quite a few very successful trips. The one session that stand out from the rest however, wasn't when I caught my personal best but when I managed to catch not one, not two but 12 double-figure bream in the same session. At this point in my angling life I had only ever caught a few 10lb-plus bream, yet I had constantly read stories of big shoals of monster bream being caught from select venues across the country. I was hoping, as every angler does, that I would one day experience such sport.

One autumn afternoon, myself and two good friends pulled into the historic Harefield car park, deep in the heart of the Colne Valley. I knew by looking at the weather that there were going to be a few fish caught but nothing prepared me for what was to come. The first night went well, with a few reasonable fish caught between the three of us but on the second evening, it all kicked off in my swim with bream after bream weighing between 10lb and just under 14lb gracing my net. Every bite had me jumping around the swim with my head in my hands and pinching myself to make sure it was really happening.

Dean with a monster bream - they're spectacular creatures when they're this big!

As the sun rose on the second morning I looked like I had been dragged through a hedge backwards. I'd had no sleep and I was covered in slime but I was grinning like a lottery winner after what was the best night's bream fishing I had ever had.

CHAPTER 8 FISHING AT NIGHT!

Night fishing can be a bit of an adventure, as well as being incredibly effective for catching many species of fish, including carp. But if you aren't properly prepared for it then it can turn into a nightmare! Often the banks will be quieter, both in terms of the number of anglers, and also the amount of disturbance that is being made by those who are still fishing!

Fishing after dark presents its own challenges, as you won't be able to see exactly what you are doing, and being organised will help to ensure that it all goes smoothly. The last thing you want to be doing for your first-ever night on the bank is to be going somewhere that you are unfamiliar with, as this will just make the whole exercise harder than it needs to be.

A good set of bite alarms are essential when night fishing.

It's a good idea to become experienced playing larger carp in daylight before you tackle a night session, just like Bobby Davro did at Old Bury Bill.

It makes good sense to go to a lake rather than a river, as flowing water can present additional problems to overcome. Choosing a venue with fairly flat banks and good access, where you can catch fish in open water, without too many snags to contend with, will also help to make the whole experience more enjoyable and something that you'll want to repeat.

If you do have any fishing friends that are already experienced at night fishing then it would be a good idea to try and tag along with one of them, rather than going on your own.

Catching fish at night can be incredibly exciting, as the darkness heightens your other senses and makes everything feel very different to what you will have experienced previously. Once you've been night fishing for a while it will become second nature and you won't even think about the fact that it is dark. If you do get a bite while you're asleep you'll probably find yourself waking up properly to find you're already playing the fish – rather than the utter panic and chaos a screaming buzzer can cause the first few times that you experience it!

Stay calm and try to avoid your other lines if at all possible. It's much easier in the light.

And talking of panic and chaos, unless you are fishing close to snags – not a good idea anyway if you're inexperienced at night fishing – you actually have far more time to get to the rod when you get a take than you might think.

A screaming buzzer can make it seem as though a fish is stripping yards of line from your reel, but rarely is that the case, and a few extra seconds won't make much difference to how far the carp runs. But it can be the difference between calmly emerging from your bivvy, lifting into the fish and being in a position to play it – as opposed to falling through the back of it, still stuck in your sleeping bag, because you panicked!

CHOOSING THE RIGHT KIT

There is a fine line between taking what you actually need to spend a night on the bank in comfort, and bringing everything, including the kitchen sink! It is inevitable that to start with you will bring loads of gear that you eventually realise that you don't actually need, and which can make setting up and packing away more of a chore than it needs to be.

But you also don't want to go to the other extreme, to find that you aren't kitted out properly and spend the night shivering and unable to sleep properly, as that could well put you off night fishing altogether! A proper bedchair is essential. Even if you think you can sleep comfortably on a low chair or similar, the

Getting the bivvy shelter and bedchair set up for the night is just one of the extra tasks to consider.

Setting your alarms correctly and making sure everything is secure is a must before settling in for the night.

A good quality head torch and spare batteries are night fishing must-haves!

reality is that you can't and will either not sleep or will wake up not being able to move your neck or back! The same goes for having some sort of shelter that offers enough protection – the days of having to fish under a 50-inch umbrella with a bin liner over the end of your bedchair to keep it dry are long gone, and there are a huge range of bivvies to choose from. A brolly with storm sides will do the job in all but the worst conditions and won't cost a fortune, or if you like a bit more comfort then there are all sorts of larger full-fronted shelters available these days.

A sleeping bag will be necessary, even in the summer, and you need to pick one that will keep you warm and comfortable in the temperatures you'll be fishing in.

Definitely go for a proper fishing one as they tend to be far roomier than the camping ones, and also have crash zips on them to allow a quick exit! Given the fact that it is going to be dark, you'll also need a source of light, which needs to be bright enough when you need to use it, but without your bivvy resembling a lighthouse and annoying everyone else around you! Tilly lamps and similar my be okay for a bit of beach fishing, but have no place in carp angling; if you do need to have a light on all the time make sure it is a dim one that isn't shining out across the lake. Really all you need is a decent headtorch - plus a spare and extra batteries - and the LED ones these days are very good, often with multiple brightness settings, and the batteries will last for ages.

Cooking on the bank can be fun and easier than you might imagine. Specialist cooking devices such as this toastie maker allow you to make surprisingly ambitious dishes!

A sandwich and a bag of crisps might be fine for a day session, but that isn't going to keep you going if you're on the bank for longer than that. Cold food works in the summer, as long as it constitutes a proper meal; but in the winter you're likely to want something hot. This means taking a stove with you, and one that is safe to use in the doorway of your bivvy. Gas is by far the safest and most hassle-free fuel source – ones that run on petrol and other fuels might be good halfway up a mountain, but are often more hassle than they're worth the rest of the time, plus getting petrol on your hands and then touching bait isn't a good idea anyway, as the fish are unlikely to be attracted to it.

To ensure that you can hit the spot you've found at night, make sure that you pick a prominent far-bank marker to line up with, like a tree or pylon.

These days the gas available to power fishing stoves is generally good enough that it will work all year round, although it might be a bit slow in the morning after a really cold night – in those conditions it is a good idea to fill your kettle the night before just in case your water bottle freezes up! The amount of cooking equipment that you take will depend on what you want to cook, and many now make do with just a toaster rather than lugging around an extra bag full of pots and pans.

Getting all of this extra kit to your swim means that you are also going to want some sort of carp barrow to save multiple trips back and forth to the car.

It pays to spend a bit more to ensure you get a good one that is stable and holds all your tackle safely and securely.

A basic kettle and stove are inexpensive and you'll appreciate a brew on colder evenings.

Measuring your line out accurately using special measuring sticks ensures an accurate cast every time.

FISHING ACCURATELY

Time spent in preparation before it gets dark will really pay off and mean that you are able to fish far more effectively. For a start if you do get a bite then you want to be able to get the rod back out accurately to the same spot, and that is easier than you might think.

You need to know which direction you are casting in and that means picking a marker on the far bank to line up with. Obviously this needs to be something permanent and also visible at night, and trees on the horizon are the best bet.

If there is nothing like that then another option is to make use of the compass on your smart phone and take a reading during daylight, although this is much harder to line up accurately in the dark – a visible marker on the horizon will draw your eye to it and your cast should automatically follow in that direction.

A strong cross wind can really mess things up as you're unable to see where your lead lands or hear where the splash is coming from, but even if you're not exactly on the spot you'll still be more accurate than just randomly chucking the rod back out!

As well as the right direction you also need to cast the right distance, and that is where measuring your lines out between two sticks set a rod length apart is essential. During daylight cast to your spot, then place the line in the clip on the spool of your reel and wind in. Then wind the line back and forth between the two sticks until you reach the clip, counting as you go, and know exactly how many rod lengths out you are fishing. Once you know that, you can either add a stop knot to your line at the right distance, or use the sticks to clip up at the right place if you do need to recast, such as after catching a fish.

Once you've measured out the distance, put the line in the clip on the spool and tie on a small length of marker elastic. When you cast out, the will be stopped when the line hits the clip, ensuring you're casting to the desired spot every time.

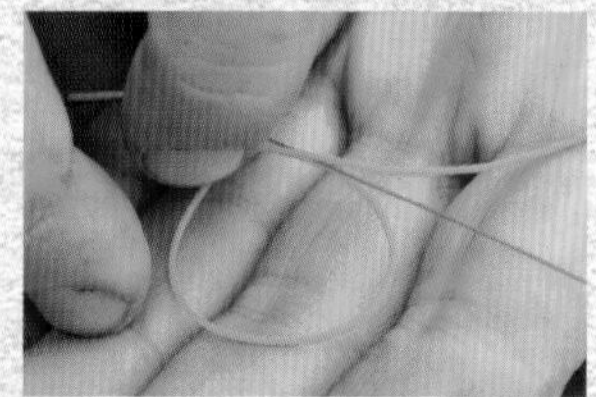

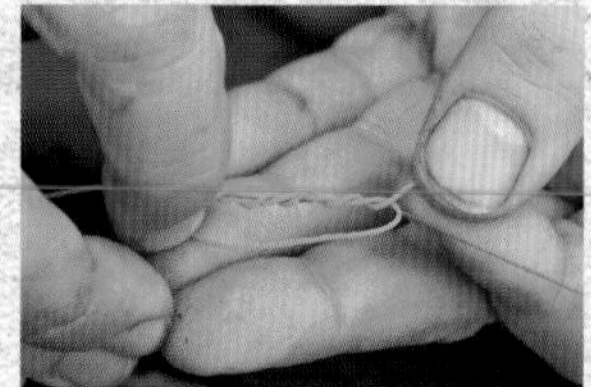

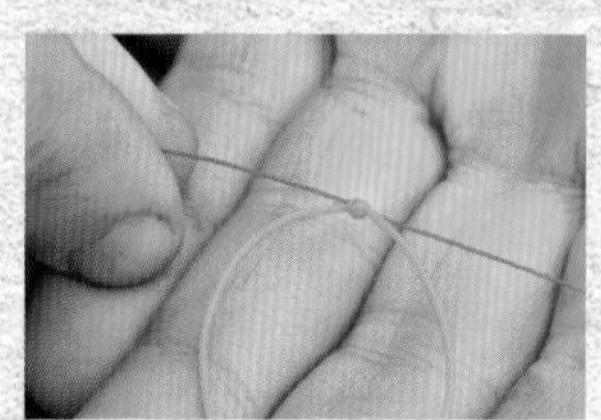

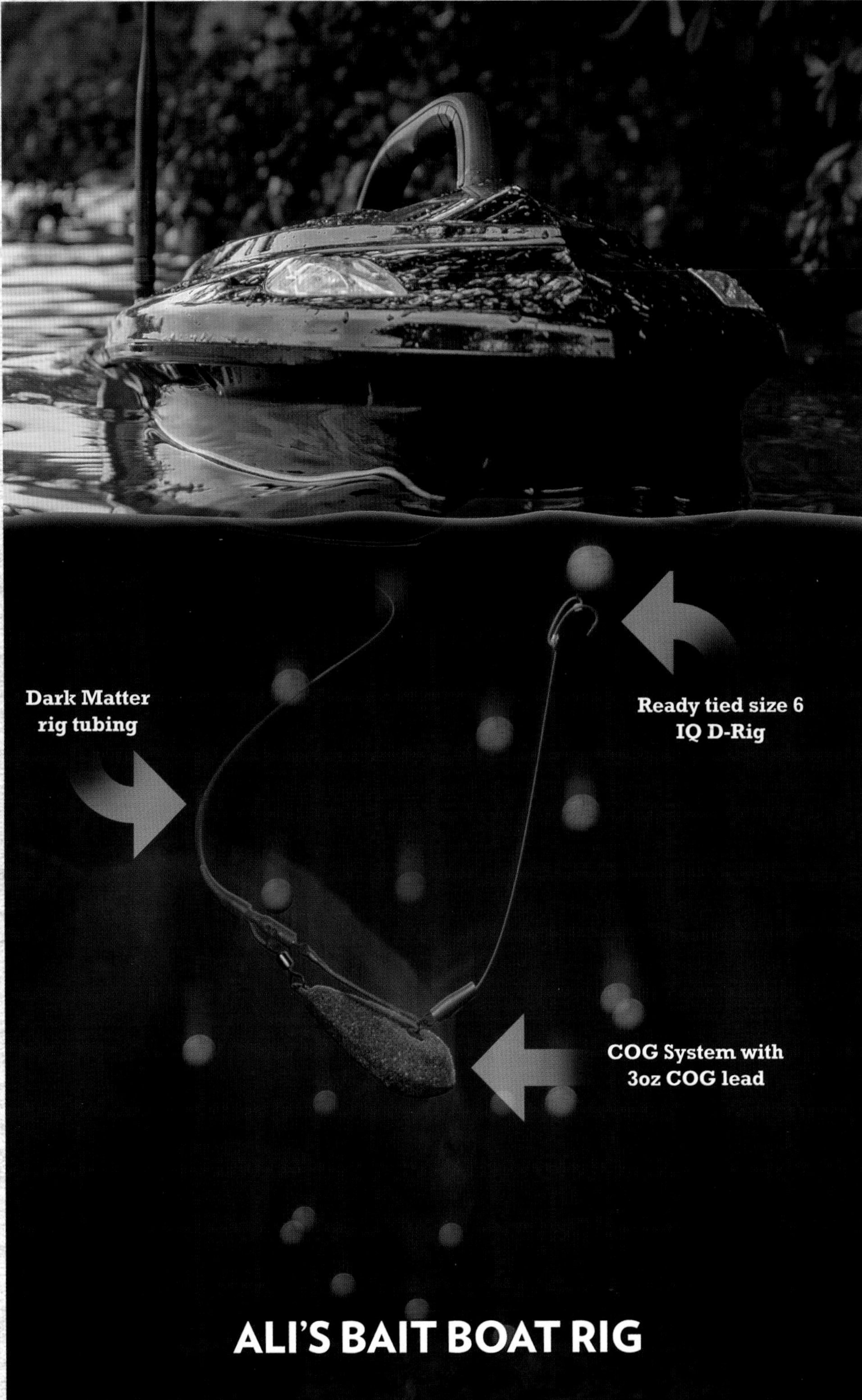
Dark Matter
rig tubing
Ready tied size 6
IQ D-Rig
COG System with
3oz COG lead
ALI'S BAIT BOAT RIG

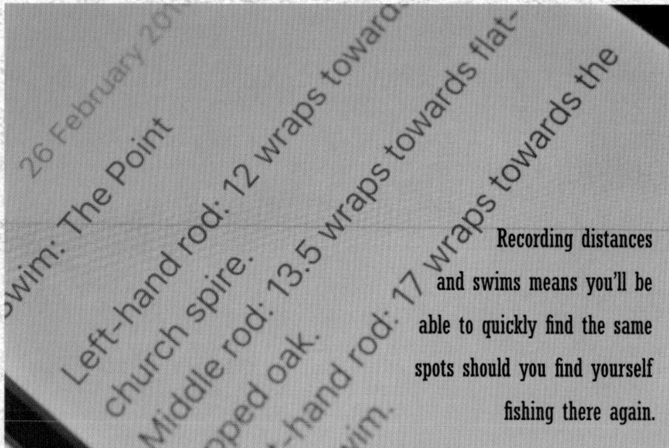

Recording distances and swims means you'll be able to quickly find the same spots should you find yourself fishing there again.

It is a good idea to store this info on your phone, especially if fishing three rods on different spots to ensure you remember it correctly. That same data could also be invaluable if you find yourself in the swim again – it even means you could turn up in the dark, such as after work for an overnight session, and get your rods out where you want them. It should make it possible to get all your rods out and then spod bait out to the spots, without actually being able to see what you're doing!

These days bait boats are an increasingly popular device for dropping a rig and bait exactly where you want it.

The top end models come with all sorts of features including an echo sounder and GPS locator, making it easy to drop your rig back in the same spot at any time of day or night, and in any conditions. But many anglers still prefer to cast their rods out rather than relying on technology, which you could argue takes a lot of the skill out of fishing.

A bait boat made in appearance in The Big Fish Off when Dean Macey and Ali Hamidi were joined by comedian Bobby Davro plus EastEnders star Ricky Groves. They were targeting carp on the Old Lake at Bury Hill Fisheries and put the boat to good use by dropping their rigs and freebies tight to overhanging trees on an island. Although both Ricky and Bobby have done a fair bit of fishing, trying to get a bait in the right spot without putting it up a tree would have been difficult without the boat, as neither guest star was all that familiar with this style of carp fishing.

Dean looks apprehensive as Bobby Davro pilots his bait boat out to their island spot...

One of the great things about bait boats is that you can deposit a neat pile of bait with your rig in the middle, tangle-free.

Season one of The Big Fish Off produced some epic overnight action for Dappy and Ollie Locke!

PLAYING FISH AT NIGHT

A carp charging about all over your swim can cause enough chaos during daylight when you can see what is going on, and in the dark can be far worse!

You need to make a mental note of any potential danger zones in your swim, be that snags in the water, big weed beds or gravel bars, so you can react to a fish heading in that direction or becoming stuck.

You can tell where a fish is heading by the feel on the rod tip, and look at the rod silhouetted against the sky to see which way the tip is bending.

BEHIND THE SCENES

During the two series of the BFO so far, a number of the challenges have involved night fishing. It has been interesting to see how the stars have reacted to spending a night outdoors, especially as some of them had little if any previous fishing experience. Some haven't exactly been keen on the idea, especially when it came to getting up during the middle of the night to land a fish. But others, such as N-Dubz music star Dappy, absolutely loved it and was quickly on the rods whenever there was a bite, although he did have the advantage of having spent a lot of time carping in the past anyway! Several of the challenges also proved how much more effective the fishing can be on some venues after dark.

Deano was over the moon with this common, which gave his team an early boost in the overnight fishing challenge!

If it is heading for a snag then you need to take action in the same way as you would during the day, by piling pressure on the fish to turn it away from danger.

Some people prefer not to use a torch when playing and netting a fish, but as long as it isn't too bright it won't be a problem and it is better to be able to see when a fish is over the net than trying to randomly scoop it up in the pitch black! What you don't want to do though is suddenly shine a bright torch on a fish as it surfaces in the margins, as it will react to that and try to charge off! Once the fish is close in you should be able to see that from the angle of your line from the rod tip to where it enters the water, plus the fish is likely to cause a disturbance on the surface. As long as there aren't any snags in the margins you can then ease off the pressure a bit once it is on a short line.

When you hook a fish you will still have anywhere from one to three other lines in the water, depending on how many rods you are using, and a kiting fish can result in all of your lines ending up in a tangled ball that is impossible to undo!

Try and keep an eye on your other rods whilst playing the fish to see if it touches any of those lines – bobbins with isotopes in are useful as you can see it move up if the line with a fish on touches another line. If the fish gets caught on one of your other lines the bobbin will drop back and the line will go slack.

You can usually avert any major tangles by passing the rod with the fish on under or over your other lines, being careful to make sure you're going the right way by checking that the other lines aren't still pulling once you've made your manouvre. If they are simply reverse the manouvre once to return the line to the previous position and again to free your lines.

We can't promise that you'll catch bigger fish by night fishing, but it's great fun, and offers a whole new world of angling adventure.

MONSTERS!

There is no reason why the fish you catch at night should be any bigger, but it can definitely give you an advantage when trying to tempt large, wary carp. On some waters there will be far less angling pressure at night, including lines in the water, which not only increases the chances of your hook bait being picked up rather than someone else's, but it also means that the fish are likely to be less cautious. It is also the time when the carp are sometimes happy to come right into the margins to feed under the cover of darkness. Night fishing can be especially effective during the warmer months when the carp can be lethargic in the heat of the day, and show little interest in feeding. Often the feeding spell will be around dawn, but by having spent the night on the bank your rigs and bait is already in place and waiting for some action – rather than turning up at that time and creating a load of disturbance getting your rods out.

If you really want to up your game and pursue carp, or even big tench, bream or eels, on difficult waters, then it's natural that you'll want to do more night fishing. For most working anglers it's the best way to make the most of the time that we have available. When the water cools in autumn and winter feeding times can switch to the middle of the night, so in order to cash in, you have to do nights! The whole process will soon become second nature and you'll stop worrying about those rustling sounds and concentrate more on pinpointing the location of night-feeding carp!

THE BIG FISH OFF GUIDE TO FISHING

CHAPTER 9 SURFACE FISHING

Walk round most lakes on a hot summer day, and you'll see big fish basking close to the surface. They're carp, and you can catch them even though they're nowhere near the lake bed! Fishing with floating bait, or surface fishing as it's known, is perhaps the most exciting of all forms of carp fishing. Apart from stalking in clear water, it's the only time that you'll actually see fish approach and take your hook bait and this sets the nerves jangling in a way that can become addictive! The visual appeal and excitement of surface fishing meant that it would simply have to feature in a BFO challenge. The two lucky guests who got to sample carping at its most instant were confirmed non-anglers, DJ Spoony and ex-pro footballer, turned TV pundit, Mark Bright. They'd learned the basics while building a mixed bag at Walthamstow, and were now ready to tackle something a little larger. If, like them, you fancy catching your first carp off the surface, then you're in luck, because we've laid out exactly how to go about it here!

About as exciting as it gets!

PICK YOUR MOMENT

As with all forms of fishing, there are times when conditions dictate that you should leave the surface kit at home. Fortunately, between the months of April and November, you can interest fish in feeding off the surface in almost all conditions. In fact, during high summer it's often the only feeding that it's possible to get carp to do, apart from in the cooler dead of night. Once the water warms up in the late spring, fish will happily feed in the surface layers.

The optimum weather conditions for surface fishing would be blue skies, and hot sun.

Naturally, the fish will be spending much of their time near the surface and can often be persuaded to feed there too. However, their appetites can be stifled by extreme temperatures, high atmospheric pressure and low oxygen levels. Cooler, overcast days can see the fish going absolutely mad for surface baits, so you should never discount a surface session during the warmer months of the year, even if the sun's not shining. Although flat-calm, dog days of summer can make for easier spotting, casting and baiting, choppier days, with some surface ripple tend to produce more bites. On a calm day, the bait sits still in the surface film, allowing carp plenty of time to regard it closely, picking out any suspicious-looking baits. When the patch of free bait is being whipped along on a ripple, the fish will find it much harder to pick out your hook bait and can snatch at baits with abandon, dropping their guard so as not to miss out on a meal.

FIVE TO TRY

Oxlease Lake, Linear Fisheries, Oxfordshire.
With fish now topping 50lb, Oxlease is right at the top of the day-ticket tree.
www.linear-fisheries.co.uk

Par Front Lake, Upminster, Essex.
A prolific floater water set amid farmland in rural Essex.
www.parfishery.co.uk

Selby Three Lakes, Selby, North Yorkshire.
A historic day-ticket water with carp to over 30lb, including some prized original fish.
www.selby3lakescomplex.com

Pine Pool, Kingsbury Water Park, Warwickshire.
Charming gravel pit with plenty of 20lb fish, in the Midlands.
www.countryparks.warwickshire.gov.uk/fishing/

Winterly Pool and Match Lake, Cheshire.
Two well-stocked lakes, which are a great bet for floater fishing.
www.winterleypool.co.uk

Mark Bright and DJ Spoony size up their surface fishing challenge in The Big Fish Off.

Believe it or not, carp can be tempted off the surface in the winter too, although a full discussion of cold-water floater fishing is perhaps best left for another day.

Suffice to say though, just like summer, high pressure systems, with their settled, clear conditions, are your best bet for spotting carp near the surface. Whether it's due to the effect of the heightened pressure, or the weak warmth from the winter sun, carp are drawn up into the surface layers at times like these. They certainly won't feed as voraciously as during the summer, but they can be caught!

CHOOSE THE RIGHT KIT

Bespoke surface-fishing kit is nice to own, but not essential if you're on a budget. In fact, you can easily make use of your main carp-fishing rods, as long as they're not too stiff or heavy! Normal carp rods of around 2.75lb are fine to use for floater fishing, given that they have enough backbone to cast the heavier inline floats, yet they're likely to be soft enough to cushion the lunges of a fighting carp and protect the light mono hook links that surface fishing demands we use in order to fool the fish. To balance a lighter rod like this you should choose a smaller reel, certainly not one of the big-pit reels that we use for bottom-bait fishing. One of the key considerations when putting together your floater fishing kit is weight. Not only will you have to carry it all around with you, moving several times a day, but for the most part, you'll be holding the rod while you're fishing, waiting for a chance to strike! As you can imagine, using a heavy rods and reel combination will mean that you're going to miss chances!

This is where the bespoke surface rods really score. They're super-light and usually have a through action, perfect for putting maximum pressure onto light hook links.

They might lack the stiffness and power that's needed to really whack out a large inline float, but they will perform admirably for 90 per cent of surface situations. The lighter your setup, the more likely that you'll still be holding it when your chance comes, and the quicker you'll be able to strike!

Ali runs Spoony through the tackle needed to catch carp off the surface.

(Top) This is the sight that all floater anglers want to see, feeding carp!

Catching carp off the surface came all too easily to Brighty! He was quick to rub it in too!

Small-but-strong Mixa hooks are ideal for surface fishing.

Reels should be loaded with 8lb or 10lb floating monofilament line, such as Korda Kruiser Line You can get away with 6lb line in waters that are totally snag free, and you may have to step up to 12lb in weedier waters. Lots of anglers choose floating braid for surface fishing these days, because braid has no stretch and transmits the force of the strike more quickly than monofilament. Hook links should be made from as thin a mono as you feel you can get away with, because this is the part of the setup that the carp will be most aware of. Thin, Japanese mono materials like Korda Zig Line and Guru N-Gauge are perfect for this job, as they're tough, yet thin and supple.

Just as with line, hooks should be as small and unobtrusive as possible – many successful anglers use hooks as small as size 12.

Carrying a range of hooks from size 6 down to 12 will cover you for all eventualities. The larger hooks can be used when weedier or snaggier conditions mean that no chances can be taken, and also for side-hooking hook baits. Korda produce a

SHOPPING LIST

- 12ft DF Floater rod
- Daiwa SS2600 Whisker reel
- 10lb Kruiser Control main line
- 10lb Zig Line or N-Gauge for hook links
- Mixa hooks
- Inline Interceptor controller floats
- Vaseline to keep hook links on the surface
- Korda Light Katapult

A reliable way of ensuring your line floats on the surface is to run it through your fingers with a blob of vaseline to coat the line as you reel in.

dedicated surface hook called the Mixa pattern, which features a super-wide gape and ultra-short shank. The real strength of these patterns are that they provide extremely assured hook holds, even thought they're relatively small hooks. The offset, wide gape and short shank combine to allow you to put lots of pressure on, without the worry of pulling the hook out. Don't be afraid of stepping down to a size-12 Mixa, even for big fish, because the wire-gauge-to-size ratio makes them extremely strong and reliable. Remember, carp will be seeing your rig from below, in silhouette, so the less conspicuous you can make your end tackle, the more likely you'll fool a carp into taking your bait. By either side-hooking or using a very short hair rig, you can ensure that the hook is hidden beneath the bait, and won't be visible against the sky when inspected.

A dash of Raspberry Plume Goo will enhance your loose feed and hook baits no end!

SURFACE TACTICS

The single biggest key to surface success is baiting. The more confidently you can get the fish feeding, the more likely it is that you'll be able to fool them into taking your hook bait. A word of warning here; it's much better to stay patient and continue feeding until the fish are gorging themselves, charging around between mouthfuls, before introducing your hook bait. If you get an itchy trigger finger and cast before the fish are confident, you risk scaring them away before your chance develops.

The longer you feed for, the more fish are likely to join the frenzy, and competition increases greed among competing fish!

Of course, it is more than possible to winkle the odd fish off the surface by casting a single hook bait into their path, but they can be rather take-it or leave-it in their attitude if they aren't already feeding. Once you have fish feeding hard, however, it is then possible to then attempt to select the fish that you want to catch by drawing the hook bait into its path as it feeds. This can be a very frustrating experience though, and selecting individual fish really is quite advanced floater fishing.

If you've managed to get fish are feeding hard, it's time to introduce the hook bait, but it's not quite as simple as that! You should always overcast, well beyond the pack of feeding carp and then slowly draw your bait back into position among them. Casting the float among the feeding fish is the surest way to spook them and ruin your chance entirely. Unless you're freelining at close range, you're going to need some weight in the setup to be able to comfortably cast beyond the fish and draw the rig back into the zone. This necessitates a float of

TOP TIP

A standard mixer biscuit or trout pellet is a fine bait in itself, but with a couple of tweaks they can be made even deadlier! First, soaking your mixers in a splash of water will add weight for catapulting out, and it'll make sure the mixer releases some of its attractive smells and taste even faster once out there. However, if you want the ultimate surface fishing bait, adding a squirt of the deadly Raspberry Plume Goo to the water before adding to the mixers and leaving them to soak for a few minutes, so they absorb the liquids, will make them nigh on irresistable to a passing carp! The concoction creates an unrivalled scent trail to pull in passing carp.

some description. There are a couple of types of floats that you might wish to consider. First up, there are inline floats, like the Korda Interceptor. These are the best all-rounders. They cast extremely well, resist tangles, and will hook fish much like a bolt rig does – meaning that you don't always have to strike, a real advantage when fishing at range and seeing that a fish has sucked in the hook bait is difficult. These inline floats range from the dinky 5g, right up to the weighty 80g, which can be cast well over 100 yards. The second style of float is a little more specialised and that's the skittle type. These are fished more like a swivel lead, running on the main line. They're great for short-range work, although they don't tend to hook fish quite as efficiently as the inlines do.

A large controller float is used for casting weight and to help set the hook. The white colour of this Interceptor model also makes it easier to spot a bite!

You'll need a catapult and spod to help you get your free baits to the where the fish are.

BAIT AND BAITING

Floating trout pellets rule the roost when it comes to surface baits, although the old favourite dog biscuits are effective too, especially when coated in fish oil. The natural oils in the pellets, or oil used to coat dog biscuits, serves to flatten the ripple around the baited patch on even quite choppy days, making it much easier to see what is happening around your hook bait. You can go for fish oils made by bait companies, such as Mainline Baits Fosoil, or for a budget option, you can coat your dog biscuits with sunflower oil from the supermarket.

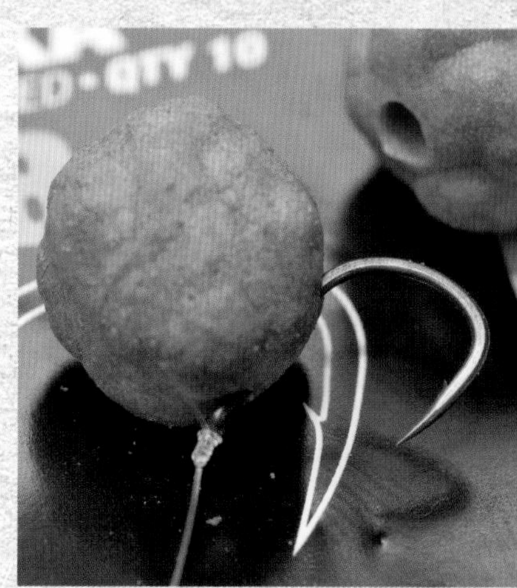

Whilst they are supremely effective at getting carp feeding, the smaller, 6mm floating trout pellets can leave the fish totally preoccupied and unwilling to so much as look at your bigger hook bait!

Imitation mixers are surprisingly effective and they last forever!

It's better to feed the larger, 11mm pellets, which are much more hook-bait sized; in fact, they can be used as hook baits themselves, but soften quickly and have a nasty habit of flying off at just the wrong moment! Dog biscuits of the mixer type tend to be around the same sort of size and can also be used on the hook. It's best to superglue dry pellets or biscuits to the back of the hook, after making a small groove in the bait to house the shank. You can't beat using the real thing in terms of fooling the fish, but once they've softened up and flown off for the fourth time you might find yourself considering other options! The best option for more robust hook baits are either fake (rubber) mixer hook baits, or pop-up boilies. Once either side-hooked or hair-rigged, these baits will stay attached and buoyant for several hours (indefinitely in the case of the rubber mixer!).

During a day's floater fishing you will need to re-bait at regular intervals to keep the fish interested and feeding. If they are within twenty yards of the bank, you can do this with a catapult. Despite the fact that the dry baits are quite light, they will fly reasonably well up to that sort of range. If you don't own a spodding setup, you can get extra range with a catapult by making up Funnelweb bags of baits, with a stone in each for extra weight. These will go thirty or forty yards and dissolve to create a little patch of bait. Beyond twenty yards, you'll have to resort to spodding or Spombing your baits out. With dedicated spodding kit, you'll be able to bait at over 100 yards, taking the bait to the fish wherever they are!

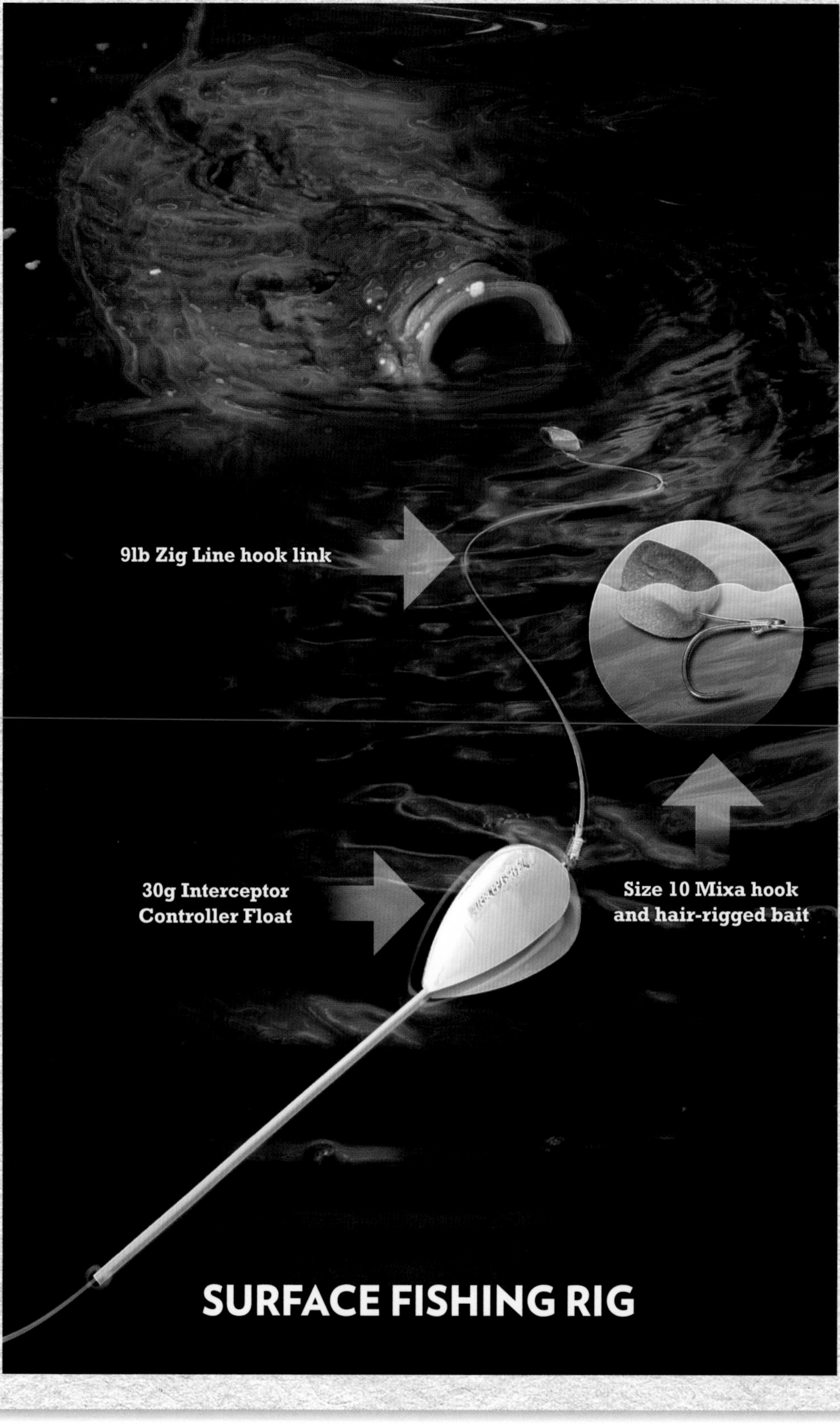

9lb Zig Line hook link

30g Interceptor Controller Float

Size 10 Mixa hook and hair-rigged bait

SURFACE FISHING RIG

A pretty mirror carp taken off the surface during The Big Fish Off.

Whether you can access small farm ponds, urban park lakes, windswept gravel pits, canals or ancient estate lakes, if they contain carp then you can catch them off the surface!

It truly is one of the most exciting forms of angling, and one that you'll enjoy immensely, if you go about it the right way. Unlike the more static carp fishing, sitting behind three rods, floater fishing can be instant and if you time it right, you can be done in a couple of hours. With minimal kit and just a single rod, you can be on the move in seconds too, keeping mind and body active while in pursuit!

THE BIG FISH OFF GUIDE TO FISHING

MONSTERS!

Richie Lofthouse broke the Norfolk record with this 52lb surface-caught giant, tempted on a classic surface bait, bread crust! He'd identified a spell of unseasonably hot weather as his last chance to trip the fish up off the surface for that particular year.

Rather than use conventional floaters, Richie fed cubes of bread because he'd noticed that the big fish had become wary of dog biscuits. "I had been feeding her all weekend and in one afternoon, she must have eaten over 100 cubes of bread!" he recalled. "I did a night in an unfancied swim because I knew it was the best area to get her feeding off the top again the next day. Sure enough, as the day warmed up, she was soon taking more of my cubes of bread. Once she was confident, I positioned my hook bait and she took it almost immediately."

Richie then battled the giant through weed, having to take to the boat to eventually land her. With the boat spinning and weed enveloping the great fish, called Babyface, Richie was able to hand-line her into the net.

Bread crust is a timeless bait that is every bit as effective today as it was when the father of modern carp fishing, Richard Walker, was fishing in the 1950s. There's just something about bread that carp just can't resist, and it's so thoroughly different to mixers and pellets that the fish may well not regard it with quite the same suspicion. It's worth using your loaf every now and again, it might just land you a monster too!

Richie Lofthouse's massive 52lb mirror caught on surface-fished bread crust. It's not just a small-fish method!

CHAPTER 10 LONG-RANGE CARP FISHING

Carp fishing has become the most popular form of coarse fishing in the UK over the last thirty years and it's not hard to see why. Carp are large, beautiful and fight hard. The scene that's grown up around their pursuit is every bit as engrossing as the fishing itself. Development of rigs, baits and hardware has been breathtaking in its speed and scope and the carp fishing industry is now bigger than ever. The carp themselves have never been so widespread, or as big. Most counties in the UK now have lakes that hold carp topping 40lb, and those holding twenties and thirties are common.

FIVE TO TRY

Layer Pit, Colchester
A famously prolific Essex water that the BFO teams caught well from. Colchester Angling Preservation Society.
www.colchesteraps.org

Brasenose One, Oxfordshire
A 32-acre day-ticket lake that holds nearly 2000 carp to well over 40lb.
www.linear-fisheries.co.uk

Big Hayes Lake, Sturminster Newton
An 8-acre day-ticket lake in Dorset with plenty of carp to mid-thirties.
www.todbermanor.co.uk

Sunnyside Two, Lancaster
A ten-acre day-ticket lake with over 160 carp in on one of the North West's most famous complexes. The lake record is 29lb.
www.wyresidelakes.co.uk

Catch 22, Lyng
A mature Norfolk gravel pit of twenty acres with lots of fish to over 40lb.
www.catch22fishingcentre.com

Historic Layer Pit in Essex was a great place to take the teams for a long-range carp challenge.

Dean has spent hours perfecting his casting technique. Could he teach Steve Collins in just a few?

With this in mind, it was natural that we'd head to some fine carp lakes for the show. One such venue is a famous Essex lake called Layer Pit. Many good anglers have cut their teeth fishing on this super-prolific water, near Colchester. Our own Ali Hamidi got to grips with carp fishing there, and it seemed like the perfect place to introduce two non-anglers to the phenomenon that is modern, long-range carp fishing!

The lads hadn't fished much before and didn't know what size of fish to expect in this challenge!

Taking two non-anglers carping might sound foolish, but that's exactly what Ali and Dean did when they teamed up with football hardman Neil 'Razor' Rudduck and former boxing world champion, Steve 'The Celtic Warrior' Collins. The question was; could they catch?

If, like the lads, you're looking to improve your carp fishing, especially at longer range, then we've got some tips for you! It'd be totally remiss of us to start without mentioning that the correct tackle is essential, if you're looking to add more than a few yards to your casting. Just as it's impossible to cast to your full potential without learning the correct technique, the best technique in the world won't balance out totally inadequate tackle!

So, what kit do you need to truly cast further? Here's our guide to getting those extra yards...

Fishing at range enabled the teams to find the larger carp, like this big common caught by Dean and Steve. The Celtic Warrior, as you might expect, bossed the fight!

RODS

Lucky you! Rods capable of helping you cast further have never been more readily available, or cheaper! For a true long-range setup you're going to need a rod of at least 3.5lb test curve. Many of the lads at Korda now use 3.75lb test curve rods for much of their fishing. If the term 'test-curve' is new to you, we can elaborate!

Basically, the higher the test curve, the stiffer the rod, and the further that it will allow you to cast... up to a point!

There's no reason to go higher than 3.75lb because the rod would become too stiff to compress properly, and too stiff to play fish on!

The more powerful rods that top companies such as Daiwa produce these days are far from the stiff broom-handles that you might expect. Instead, they're forgiving tools that allow you to play fish without the worry of hook pulls once you have them under the rod tip – often the critical moment! If your budget for long-range rods is tight, then you needn't despair. Plenty of companies make long-range tools for those watching the pennies, and these rods, although cheaper, will serve you well. Opting for a 13ft rod, rather than the conventional 12ft version will add distance to your casting. They are marginally less versatile though, so if you can only afford one set of rods, stick with the 12-footers!

Dean is an expert caster and his skills were put to good use in this challenge.

BASIA45

If you're going to be fishing at long range, you'll benefit from using big-pit reels, like Dean's Basias. They hold lots of line and the large coils that they let off during the cast help get extra range.

REELS

So-called big-pit reels still rule the roost for long-range fishing. They hold lots of line, and their wide spool rim allows the line to whisper off in large coils, reducing drag and aiding your casting. Smaller reels, especially the new generation of so called baby-big-pit reels (models like Daiwa's Cast'izm), are also well suited to long-range fishing and in casting tests they hold their own alongside their big brothers.

Once again, the sky really is the limit in terms of cost – you can pay an eye-watering amount for three top-end big-pit reels. You'll be getting the absolute cutting-edge in terms of materials and these futuristic models tend to be incredibly light, shaving plenty of weight off your setup, which will help you move that rod faster and cast further than ever!

However, just like the rods, there are some fabulous, reliable big-pit reels available for well under £100 each – particularly in the Emblem stable at Daiwa.

Spodding at long range calls for thin braided main line and a robust braided leader.

Darrell Peck's long-range rig is simple and won't tangle. He's caught some massive carp on it, too!

END TACKLE

Having got yourself set up with the right rods and reels, you need to turn your attention to the line and end tackle that will help you make the most of your new kit! Perhaps the most important element in your long-range setup is main line, and most anglers turn to monofilament for this, although some prefer super-thin performance braids. Simply put, the thicker and heavier it is the less far you can cast it. For the very best distance performance, 10lb main line is about right. However, you can't give this line the big heave-ho safely without a length of stronger line, called a leader, which will absorb the power of the cast, preventing the line snapping when you accelerate through. These events, called crack-offs, occasionally happen when you're going all-out, but you should do everything in your power to avoid them, as they're dangerous and frankly, extremely inconvenient!

You have two main options when it comes to leaders: individual tapered mono leaders, which you tie to your main line, or tapered main line, which tapers in the last 15 metres from a thinner diameter to a thicker leader section (no leader knots needed). Both of these tapered leader options feature thick, strong line at the lead end, which then tapers smoothly down to a much thinner, casting line thickness. Because there are no knots needed, we'd recommend the tapered main line to start with! If you're unlucky enough to lose the tapered section, you can simply reverse the line onto a spare spool, revealing another identical tapered section at the other end of the line! For optimum casting potential, you can cut the tapered section down from 15 metres to 8 metres, to reduce drag once airborne.

Keep your rigs and terminal tackle streamlined to ensure it stays tangle-free and effective.

A tapered line features a thick casting leader, tapering down to a thin main line – allowing easier distance casting.

A stiff fluorocarbon rig is also a great option for tangle-free distance fishing, especially for big carp!

Long-range fishing is not the discipline in which to deploy complicated rigs. The potential for tangles is slightly greater, given the forces and distances involved, so simple really is best. Darrell Peck has developed a reputation as one of the best long-range anglers in the UK. His terminal setup simply incorporates some heavy rig tubing, a lead clip and a simple, tangle-resistant rig. Of course, you'll need a suitably large lead for long-range fishing, and Distance Casting leads in 3.5oz are a great place to start. By all means, build up to using 4oz leads as your long-range casting technique improves, but many find it easier to start slightly lighter!

Sloppy groundbait, mixed with Goo got the carp searching in the upper layers.

Blasting zig rigs out to long range proved to be the best tactics at Layer, and the lads followed up their little foam hook baits with a good helping of Goo-infused sloppy spod mix! By introducing a smelly cloud of ground bait that sits in the water column around the hook bait, the teams were able to concentrate the carp's attention around their baits, which proved extremely productive. The cloud dispersed far and wide, drawing more fish into the zone, which the lads kept topped up. As so often happens in this situation, the sloppy spod mix that made it to the lake bed starts to pull fish down to it, through the layers, and the carp began to bubble profusely over the hempseed and groundbait that had settled!

Should this happen to you; a quick switch to a bottom-bait setup will usually bring rewards!

LONG-RANGE ZIG-RIG TACTICS!

The teams started their Layer session using zig-rig tactics, because both Ali and Dean knew that the fish would respond to sloppy spod mix. The Layer fish are renowned for homing in on spodded areas, and when you introduce a mix that clouds the water and lingers, the fish will come up through the water, towards the surface, much as they would when feeding on hatching insects.

To take advantage, you need to present your hook bait in amongst the sloppy cloud, right where the fish are searching. Smearing the hook bait with Goo offers another level of attraction that will draw fish to your hook bait quickly. Both Ali and Dean set up their lead clip systems to drop the leads, which is essential for zig-rigging. Because the zig hook links are so long, the last thing you need is to have a big lead swinging around near the rod tip when you're drawing the fish close to the net.

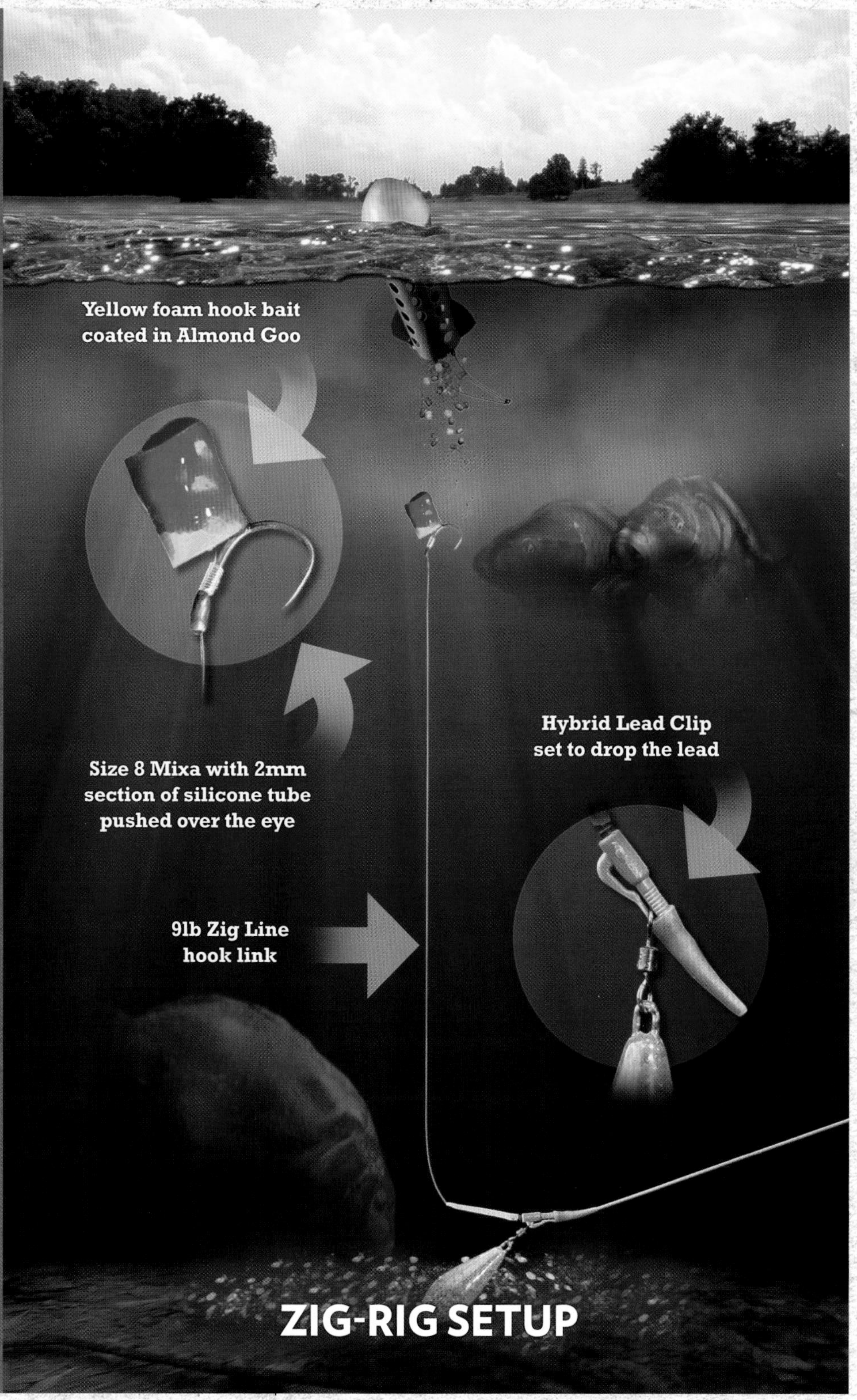

Yellow foam hook bait coated in Almond Goo

Size 8 Mixa with 2mm section of silicone tube pushed over the eye

Hybrid Lead Clip set to drop the lead

9lb Zig Line hook link

ZIG-RIG SETUP

BEHIND THE SCENES

Long-range casting is a skill that requires serious practice so, given that neither Neil or Steve had cast a fishing rod before (at least not since they were teenagers… a long time ago!), the captains were allowed to cast out for them. Both Ali and Dean are expert casters and capable of launching a lead and rig well over 120 yards, Dean also regularly practices on his local playing field to keep his casting skills sharp. Fishing at Layer demanded accuracy and consistency on the cast, which simply wouldn't have been fair on our two newbies, so they just got to reel 'em in and they made a great job of doing just that!

Baiting up at long range takes some thought. Throwing sticks are great for baiting up to around the 100 yard mark with boilies, and they can be used to bait up further still, with heavy, hardened baits and great technique. However, the best way (in fact, the only way for particles or sloppy spod mix) to introduce bait at extra-long range is to use a spod or a Spomb. When loaded, these baiting tools can weigh a lot more than a normal rig. That means you need specialised kit to cast them.

Dean and Ali both kept their swim topped up regularly with Spomb or spod fulls of bait.

If you're introducing light food items, then you'll need a spod to do it!

Powerful spod rods and quick-retrieve spod reels, loaded with the latest super-thin Spod Braid, will allow you to bait around your rigs up to 160 yards, and beyond. Once again, a shock leader is absolutely vital, although this time a braided leader, such as Arma-Korda in 30lb is best.

If you use a braided line of any description, it's critical that you protect your casting finger with a neoprene fingerstall, and screw the clutch on your reel down so that it cannot yield line on the cast. Failing to do either of these things can lead to severely cut fingers!

Locating carp, and suitable spots to fish at long range is every bit as critical as anywhere else you might fish. When pressured, carp will often move out to the middle of the lake, especially if there is no weed or snags for them to hide in elsewhere. Once out of the range of most anglers, the fish often feel comfortable enough to feed freely. Signs that they're feeding out in the lake are the same anywhere – bubbling, rolling, crashing and head-and-shouldering are the prime giveaways! Should you find fish doing this, it can be worth casting single hook baits at them as they feed, but far more cunning is to wait for them to stop (assuming you have the time), before researching the spot that they are feeding on with a marker rod setup. This will give you an insight as to the type of lake bed that's out there, and the rigs that you need to choose as a direct result.

ARMA
KORD
50lb
22kg/20m
ABRASION RESISTANT
BRAIDED LEADER

Once Steve had got the hang of playing the carp, he really started to enjoy it! Who can blame him, when the carp look as good as this fully scaled mirror?

Your maker float setup should be every bit as powerful as your spodding kit, so that you can reach the areas that you plan to fish. Thin, braided main lines like Korda Marker Braid coupled with Arma-Kord leaders will give you the confidence to really hit that float setup hard! The braids have zero stretch, which allows you to feel every bump as you slowly pull the lead back towards you across the area of lake bed that you want to investigate. If you find a nice smooth area of silt, clay or sand (this will feel like the lead is pulling across a sheet of glass), or some clean gravel (you will feel the lead 'juddering' across the stones), then it can often be worth popping the float up and marking the spot because there's every chance that the fish have kept the spot clear, thanks to their feeding activity. Now, having done the hard work, casting around the swim to find a clear area, you mustn't lose it! Make a careful note of the direction your float is in.

The best way to do this is to line it up with a permanent horizon marker, such as a tall tree, pylon or church tower! This way, whether night or day, you can step into the swim and cast to your spot without needing to get the marker float out again.

A strong braided leader is essential for casting large Spombs and spods any sort of dustance. Remember to use a finger stall!

With the float popped up, and the horizon marker noted, you need to record how far out your spot is. Using one of your fishing rods, with the rig removed, cast to the float and feel the lead impact the lake bed by trapping the line and letting it swing down on a tight line. Following the lead with your rod tip ensures that it sinks on a straight line and amplifies the 'feel' of the impact. The way the lead impacts the bottom will tell you whether you're on the spot that your float is marking or not (gravel will register as a sharp tap or bang, clay and sand as a firm thud and silt as a soft thud). Over water, it's easy to misjudge exactly where your lead is landing in relation to your float, so keep trying until you get it right, using the line clip on your reel to ensure that you can recast exactly to the spot every time.

Finally, using a pair of distance sticks set a rod length apart (use bank sticks if you don't have them), with your lead at the foot of one stick, wrap your line around the two until you hit the clip. Counting the wraps as you make them will allow you to replicate the distance every time!

Being accurate with their baiting and casting allowed Dean and Steve to build up a great run of sizeable fish.

Keeping detailed records of spots and distances allows you to find the same hotspot again in no time!

Wrapping your line around two distance sticks, set a rod-length apart, will help you record the range you're fishing at.

Once you've mastered the specialised techniques involved with going that bit further than usual, you'll have added a vital string to your bow.

Long-range carp fishing is by no means a guarantee of success, but when the fish move out to long range, it is the only way to catch them and lots of anglers simply can't do it effectively! Far too often though, those who can, fall into the trap of fishing way past the carp, because range fishing is so absorbing in its own right! Follow our advice and find the fish first, whether they're at 160 yards, or right under your feet, rather than deciding where to fish before you even pull into the car park! If the carp are sitting out at long range, you'll now be perfectly equipped to fish long, fish accurately and catch them!

A zig rig is really simple, consisting of a small cylinder of foam or pop-up boilie hair-rigged to a mono hook link.

DID YOU KNOW?

It's not known for sure when zigging emerged as a technique in carp fishing. Fishing buoyant baits such as bread crust anchored on a long hook link had been used since carping's dim-and-distant past, but zigging has become something of an art form over the last decade! It's widely speculated that the technique was developed at Devon Mecca, Angler's Paradise, which is owned by eccentric angler, Zyg Gregorek. Having pioneered the method, the name stuck… kind of! Perhaps it should be called Zygging?

LONG-RANGE MONSTERS
DARRELL PECK

There's a satisfaction in hitting just the right spot, at extreme range that is hard to beat. It's especially hard to beat when it leads to a big carp on the bank too! I had to learn to up my long-range game when I tackled a huge water on the South Coast, Rockford. I was able to locate the carp fairly quickly, thanks to seeing a few shows. They were held up right out in the middle, in a zone that nobody could reach. By kitting myself out to get as close to the area as I could, I had one of the best winters ever, which was capped off with the capture of one of my biggest-ever fish, Single Scale at 57lb.

Those fish knew that they were safe out in the middle, but when they ventured a little closer, I'd catch a few, which made the casting practice that I'd had to do all the more worthwhile!

I was able to take what I'd learned at Rockford and apply it to fishing in a similar situation in Belgium for the Korda Masterclass Vol. 2 DVD. By fishing and baiting at longer range than most people were able to, I gained a huge advantage and was able to capitalise. Of course, you have to know those fish are out there, but once you do, you can take some great catches. I certainly benefitted from plenty of practice and, I'm not afraid to say it, watching tuition films from expert long-range carper Mark Hutchinson. You're never too old to learn from the best!

Learning to cast and bait at range can be a huge advantage over rival anglers, and wary carp!

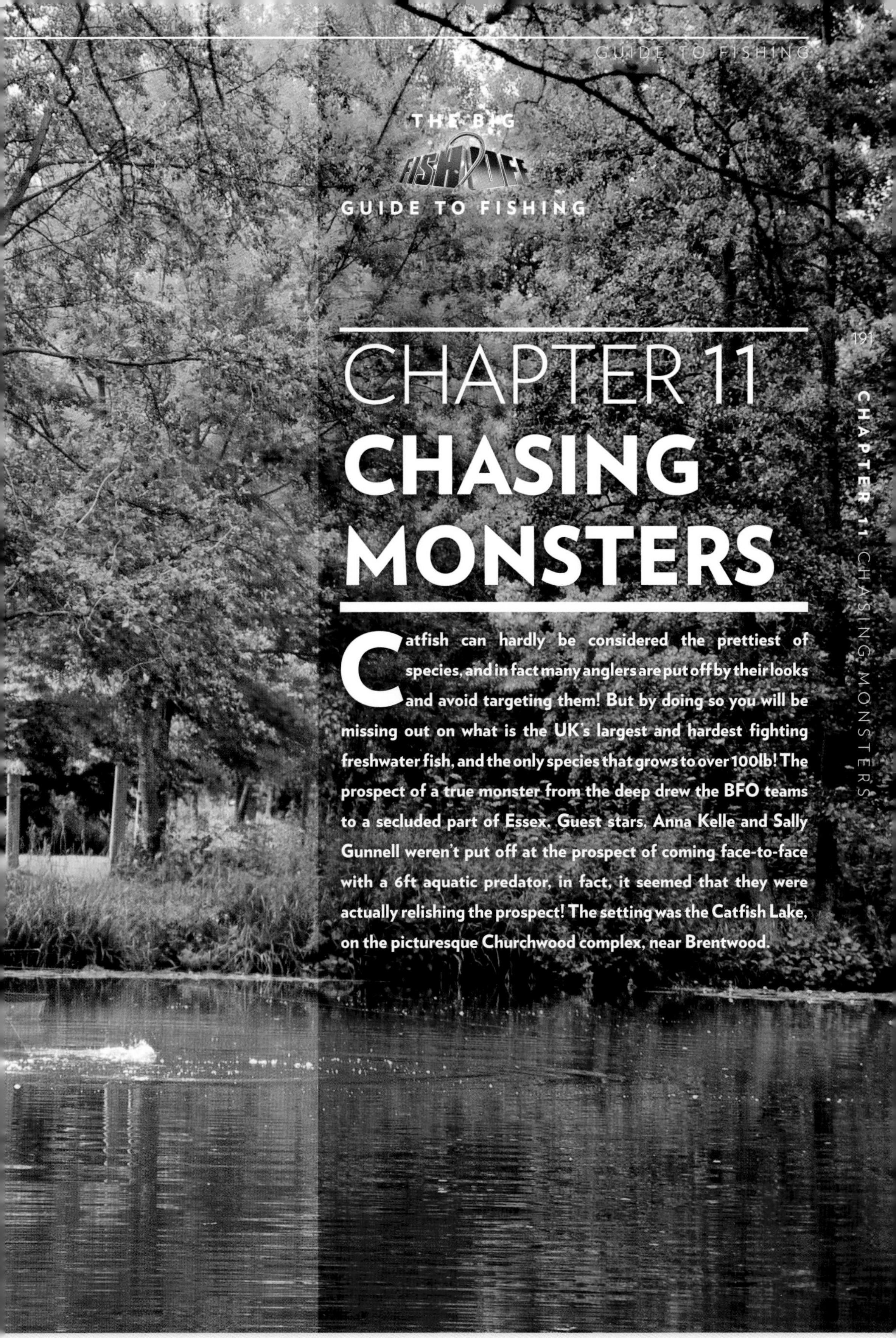

THE BIG FISH OFF
GUIDE TO FISHING

CHAPTER 11 CHASING MONSTERS

Catfish can hardly be considered the prettiest of species, and in fact many anglers are put off by their looks and avoid targeting them! But by doing so you will be missing out on what is the UK's largest and hardest fighting freshwater fish, and the only species that grows to over 100lb! The prospect of a true monster from the deep drew the BFO teams to a secluded part of Essex. Guest stars, Anna Kelle and Sally Gunnell weren't put off at the prospect of coming face-to-face with a 6ft aquatic predator, in fact, it seemed that they were actually relishing the prospect! The setting was the Catfish Lake, on the picturesque Churchwood complex, near Brentwood.

TOP FIVE CATFISH WATERS

Lakemore Fisheries, near Crewe, Cheshire
The complex record stands at over 75lb and there are lots in the 20-30lb range.
www.lakemorefisheries.co.uk

Churchwood Fishery, Brentwood, Essex
The Catfish Lake may only be small but it has a good head of 30s, 40s and even 50s.
www.churchwoodfisheries.co.uk

Orchid Lakes, Dorchester, Oxfordshire
Club Lake is only around two acres in size but is home to a good head of catfish, with three of them topping the 50lb mark.
www.orchid-lakes.co.uk

Shatterford Lakes, Kidderminster, Worcestershire
These mature lakes are renowned for their catfish in the local area, with specimens now running to over 70lb.
www.shatterfordlakes.com

Oakwood Park Lakes, Thetford, Norfolk
A day-ticket fishery that's home to the largest catfish in the UK, with fish to over 120lb!
www.oakwoodparklakes.co.uk

Dean sets out to place a catfish bait into a likely looking area at Churchwood with the aid of a boat.

Dean and Ali with Churchwood owner Steve Sands (below)

The wels catfish (Silurus glanis) is a relative newcomer to the UK, having only been introduced 130 years or so ago when the Duke of Bedford stocked 70 of them into the lakes at Woburn Abbey. For many years it was only really a handful of lakes around that area of Bedfordshire that held cats, and in terms of their size, a fish over 30lb was considered big.

Things have changed dramatically over the last 15 years, and there are now waters in almost every county in England with cats in them.

They are still considered a non-native species so these venues need a licence to keep them and can only be stocked into lakes that aren't close to rivers, where there is a danger of them escaping. It would seem a bit late for that however, as catfish have been caught in a number of rivers, including the Thames, Severn and Great Ouse, as well as the Grand Union Canal. That said, they still aren't common in flowing water when compared to the large European river systems.

BEHIND THE SCENES

The Big Fish Off paid a visit to Churchwood Fishery, in Brentwood, Essex, to see if they could catch some catfish for the cameras. Presenters Dean Macey and Ali Hamidi were joined by former Olympic athlete Sally Gunnell and reality TV star and celebrity photographer Anna 'AK' Kelle. The girls got a shock when they found out they'd have to spend all night on the bank for this 24-hour challenge to catch the biggest catfish! Fishing baits suspended off of the bottom, they had to wait until after dark for the bigger cats to go on the feed, with both Sally and AK being woken up in the middle of the night to play fish. Sally got to feel the power of a bigger cat first when she landed one of over 25lb, and was left gasping: "My wrist! My arm! It's really hard work but so exciting. I absolutely loved it and now I can say that I can actually fish." This was great to see, as AK in particular hadn't been overly impressed by the looks of a catfish or how slimy it was, and took some convincing that she did actually want to hook one!

Camping by a lake whilst fishing for huge, slimy wels wasn't the girls idea of fun, until both Sally and AK hooked into big catish!

In the flesh they are far more impressive than they appear to be in any photo, and despite their looks there is something quite appealing about this sleek, powerful species – although they are quite slimy!

They are also generally fairly well behaved on the bank if handled properly, and all of the fight tends to be in the water rather than when you're trying to hold one for a photo. The long, sleek shape means that this fish is a powerful fighter, and whilst the tail might not resemble the large paddle that is found on species such as carp, you shouldn't let that deceive you, as the whole back end of a catfish is pure muscle! When hooked it will charge all over the lake, often going on searing, unstoppable runs that leave you just hanging on and praying that it will stop before it finds a snag.

There are now plenty of waters where they have grown to over 70lb. Fish of this size don't give up easily and can sometimes take 30 minutes or more to land, especially in larger waters where they have the space to really fight. Wherever you live you should be able to find somewhere reasonably close that gives you a chance of catching one of these beasts, and it is really just a case of picking the type of water that you want to fish.

Many catfish are found in smaller lakes, often as part of a day-ticket complex, where there are a good head of fish and you have a reasonable chance of catching. But there are also larger, low-stocked venues out there, which offer a real challenge. The famous Tring Reservoirs complex is a prime example, a venue that once held the British record with a fish of 43lb 8oz, caught back in 1970 (that fish is still on display today in Tring museum).

Dusk is prime time for big catfish!

STRONG TACKLE

The gear you need to land a catfish will depend on the size of fish that you are targeting and the type of venue you're on. If you're unlikely to hook anything bigger than 50lb, and the lake is mostly snag-free and open water, then normal carp tackle, such as 3lb test curve rods and 15lb main line, will suffice. For anything bigger than that, or on venues where you might need to try and stop a fish from getting around the back of an island or extracting it from a weed bed, you will need to step up to something heavier. These days, there are specialist catfish rods available, and something of around 4lb test curve is about right, or at a push you could get away with a 3.5lb pike rod.

The main thing is that it is through-action, or at least has a soft enough tip to absorb the lunging fight of a cat. Long-range carp rods in heavier test curves don't tend to have the right action, being too stiff.

Big pit style reels are perfect for this sort of fishing, as they hold plenty of heavier line and are robust, but you definitely want to pick one that has a free-spool system. Catfish can be wary of resistance when they pick up a bait, especially larger baits, and a free-spool system is perfect, as it quickly allows you to go from freespool to your chosen clutch setting. Don't make the mistake of thinking that you can play a big catfish using backwind, as when it goes on a run you won't be able to keep up and you need a correctly set drag instead!

You can use braid or monofilament main line, but you need something that is strong enough, and that will mean at least 20lb nylon - although you don't want to go heavier than you need to otherwise you'll struggle to fit enough on, even these big

Tough main line is essential, we'd suggest 20lb monofilament or 50lb braid, such as Apex.

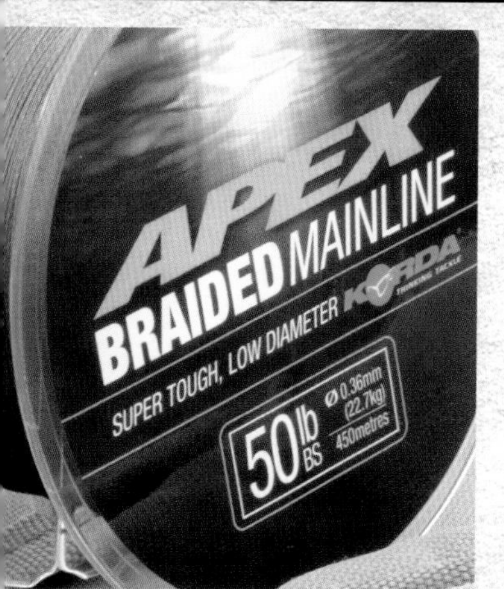

reels. If you are going to use braid it is a good idea to go for something of 60lb test or stronger. That might seem a bit over-the-top, but braid is much thinner than mono, and as well as the strength you also want the abrasion resistance that comes with a heavier, thicker braid.

Single banksticks are a good idea as it means that you can point your rods directly at the bait, as like most predators, catfish are wary of resistance.

A bobbin that easily comes off of the line will reduce the chances of a dropped take – although with smaller baits the takes tend to be screamers anyway and resistance isn't really a concern.

RIGS AND BAITS

There are a wide variety of rigs and baits that will catch catfish, everything from boilies, pellets, and luncheon meat through to worms, leeches, squid and dead fish.

A standard setup for many catfish waters would be a couple of large boilies or halibut pellets fished on a hair rig, basically a heavy-duty version of a carp rig. This would be fished with a running lead, ideally fished on some sort of lead link with a run ring to ensure that it is resistance free.

Catfish don't have teeth, but what they do have are sharp, rasping pads on the inside of their mouth, and these can quickly wear through standard braided hook link materials, so you need something heavier and tougher, such as a snag leader material or a purpose-designed catfish hook link in 45lb or heavier. Heavier mono and fluorocarbon are also suitable for some rigs.

Wels catfish have huge mouths with abrasive pads on their top and botom jaw, used for grasping onto prey.

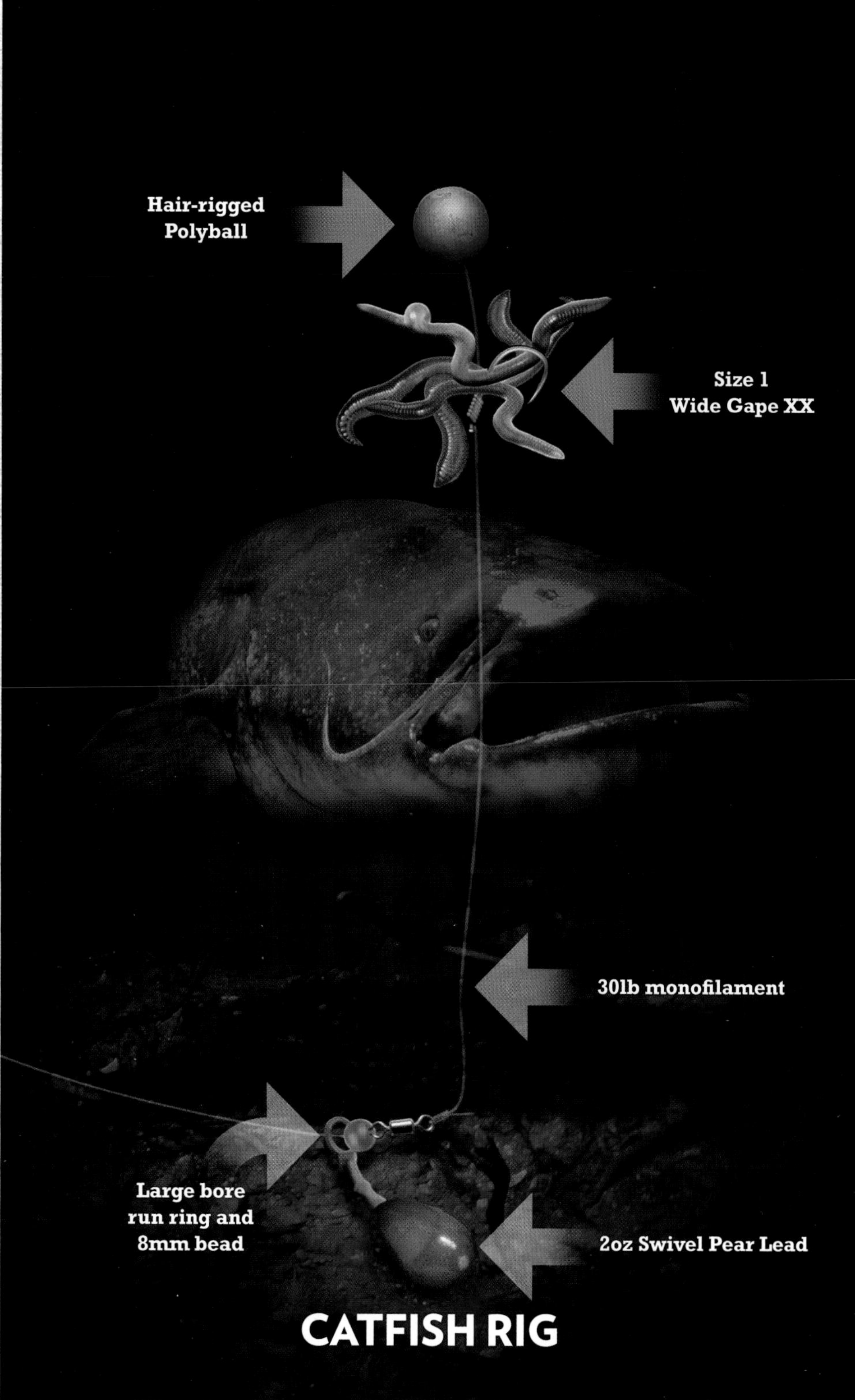
Hair-rigged
Polyball
Size 1
Wide Gape XX
30lb monofilament
Large bore
run ring and
8mm bead
2oz Swivel Pear Lead
CATFISH RIG

Hooks also need to be stronger and bigger than those you use for carp, starting at a size 1 or 2 for this type of boilie or pellet setup, and even larger if you're using a bigger bait, especially when side-hooking, rather than using a hair. Fishing on the bottom like this is the easiest way of targeting catfish, and you simply need to feed a load of pellets and/or boilies over the top, along with anything else smelly, such as groundbait, that might get the attention of a catfish.

Cats don't just feed on the bottom though, and will take baits presented at any depth, including on or just below the surface, especially at night.

Catfish have an exceptional sense of smell – use this to your advantage with some seriously pungent bait, such as these fishmeal pellets, to attract the cats to the area.

Adding oily fish such as tins of tuna is a great way to attract hungry catfish to your baited area.

A close-up view of a catfish rig that we'd recommend for novice anglers.

This leads to all sorts of different presentations that are designed to either pop a bait up using buoyant polyballs, or to suspend it just below the surface using a dumbbell rig, which floats on top of the water. You may have to vary the depth that you fish your rigs at until you get action from cats.

This type of rig would usually be used with something like a big bunch of worms, which give off vibrations as they squirm around, or a chunk of dead fish to give off lots of smell – cats have terrible eyesight so tend to rely on smell and vibration to hunt their food.

Not all catfish are huge! This wels is a baby compared to its bigger brothers and sisters that live at Churchwood.

DID YOU KNOW?

Catfish will eat pretty much anything and although considered to be a predator, the wels is more of a scavenger. They will chase and eat live fish - or even wildfowl, frogs and rats - using their whiskers to sense exactly where the prey is and then engulf it in their huge mouth, with the sharp pads preventing any chance of escape. However, they are also just as happy to eat dead fish and animals lying on the lake bed, or any other source of food that they can find, such as angler's bait. One of the reasons that they are able to fight so hard is due to their ability to swim backwards – one of only a handful of species, including eels, that have this ability. This can make them very hard to land and is why you need a suitable sized net or they'll swim out of it backwards if it isn't large enough to scoop the whole fish up and its tail is left hanging out! Catfish tend to either be in feeding mode or not, with not much in the way of middle ground, with factors such as weather conditions and moon phase triggering these feeding frenzies. When they are on the feed anglers all around the lake are liable to be getting bites, but when they switch off there is often nothing that you can do to tempt one.

Catfish require large, soft unhooking mats and specialist slings.

FISH CARE

Due to their shape, standard carp care equipment isn't really suitable – even a 20lb catfish is longer than a 50lb carp! You are going to need a net with at least 50-inch arms, and for bigger cats one of the purpose-made catfish nets of 60 inches or larger will be necessary if you're going to have any chance of getting your catch to fit in it. The same applies to unhooking mats, and if you don't have a proper catfish model then you can get away with two carp mats side by side. Even the largest of carp slings will still see a larger cat hanging out of either end of it, so make sure your weigh sling is long enough.

You're also going to need a bigger set of scales than you might already have, depending on the size of fish being targeted, and some sort of tripod to hang them from.

The easiest way of maneuvering a catfish when it is on the mat is to grip it just inside the bottom jaw with four of your fingers – there is a groove just behind the pad – and with your thumb outside under the jaw. A glove is a good idea otherwise the sharp pads can cut your skin.

MONSTER CATFISH!

In the UK catfish have been caught to well over 100lb, although there is no official record, as they aren't classed as a native species. Because of their length, even fish that are much smaller than that can still look very impressive in the flesh, as was seen on the Big Fish Off when AK hooked into one of the bigger specimens in Churchwood. It was no record-breaker but you could see the strain as she played it in until fishing partner Ali Hamidi was able to get the net under it, and it turned out to be the biggest of the session at 46lb 8oz! Once she'd recovered, she enthused: "I didn't think I'd catch a fish at all. It was amazing – ugly but amazing. I think I need some painkillers for my back now!"

THE BIG
FISH'N'LIFE
GUIDE TO FISHING

CHAPTER 12 LET'S GO SEA FISHING!

As an island nation, we're surrounded by several seas containing a wealth of fish; from colourful inshore wrasse, blennys and mackerel to the famed cod and skate the boys target in The Big Fish Off. Fishing in the sea can be more challenging than freshwater, but it can also be really simple and fun if you have the right skills, knowledge and tackle. Join the lads as they run through some basic sea fishing skills during their voyage with an expert skipper off the East Coast - ahoy there Neil 'Razor' Ruddock and Steve 'The Celtic Warrior' Collins!

Getting afloat on a professionally-run charter fishing boat is a safe and enjoyable way of starting sea fishing.

Our seas are full of fish that you can catch on rod and line, from tiny rockpool-dwelling species to massive sharks. In-fact, sharks are one of the most plentiful fish species in the UK, with at least 30 different species living in our seas, ranging from small dogfish that will pick up baits meant for cod, to monster porbeagle, mako and thresher sharks. Huge basking sharks are also resident but they're too big to catch on rod and line, plus they only eat plankton. You may have seen them if you've been on a whale watching trip to Cornwall or Scotland.

Skate are also commonly called rays, and they're a member of the shark family. They share the shark's tough skin, which is actually made up on millions of tiny scales made from a material similar to teeth and bones – this makes them hard for predators to eat. You also have to be careful when handling skate, dogfish and other sharks as the tough skin has the texture of sandpaper and can remove your skin if you're not careful. A firm grasp holding the tail to its head in one hand won't hurt it and will make sure the skin doesn't rub against yours. A thornback ray, the species the lads caught in the show, also has small spines along its back which are just like the thorns found on a rosebush, hence the name. Be very careful when handling these! Other types of ray found in the UK include the blonde and undulate ray.

Both cod and skate grow to well over 20lb in British waters and they're now relatively plentiful following restrictions on commercial fishing, making them a great target if you fancy a day on a boat. That said, you don't need to take fish you catch from the sea home to eat and we'd always advocate only taking what you really need and carefully returning everything else.

So for your next Big Fish Off challenge, we're going to teach you how to catch your first sea fish from a boat!

FIVE TO TRY

Bridlington, East Yorkshire
A famous fishing port on the North East coast for centuries! Call North Bay Angling on 84 Promendade, Bridlington on 01262 401144.

Bradwell Marina, Bradwell on Sea, Essex.
John Rawle runs his charter boat from Bradwell Marina and is your man for East coast action! Call 01621 776445 / 07860 920 964 or go to www.johnrawlefishing.co.uk

Hayling Island, Portsmouth, Hampshire
This south coast island is a great place to get a charter boat from. Call Solent Tackle in Portsmouth for information on 02392 739116.

Newquay, Cornwall
A great holiday destination with lots of local sea fishing opportunities from boat and shore. Try a shore mark called Fly Cellars for small species on float tackle!

Holyhead, North Wales
Much like the rest of Wales, Holyhead is a mecca for sea angling with an emphasis on the larger species. Call local expert Gethyn Owen on 07971 924046 or go to www.goangling.co.uk

A boat is the perfect place to start sea fishing because the skipper, or captain, will be able to guide you and position the boat in a prime position for you to hopefully catch lots of fish. Casting from a beach or seafront is a lot harder and requires specialist equipment, although dropping a rig from the side of a pier is an easy and cheap option and there are lots of piers that allow fishing.

The lads prepare for a day at sea. Would there be any casualties? Dean was particulary worried as he had previous form for sea-sickness.

It all got too much for Steve!

Lots of ports around the UK offer charter boat trips – some of the best are listed in this chapter – and local tackle shops or sea angling clubs will be able to recommend a boat or skipper. Some even do special evening trips in the summer for mackerel or bass – this is a great way of getting a taste of sea fishing or for youngsters with short attention spans! Another advantage of going with a reputable skipper is that they'll often provide tackle and bait, so you just have to turn up and fish.

For the sea fishing challenge in The Big Fish Off, which saw footy hardman Neil 'Razor' Ruddock take on Irish boxing legend Steve Collins, the lads had the benefit of being in the hands of one of the best skippers in the business – sea fishing legend John Rawle.

Essex-based John invented his own form of sea fishing – uptiding, where the rig is cast from the boat and presented away from the boat – and is a legend of the sea angling world. What John doesn't know about sea fishing isn't worth knowing!

A real expert, John started out sea fishing when he was very young: "I got into fishing when I was four and started going with my Dad. My first fish was a flounder of about 1lb caught off Southend Pier - I showed everyone who walked past! It turned out that dad wanted to do more saltwater than fresh at the time, so I got into sea fishing."

Cod are one of the most prized species to be caught around the British Isles – but they're not all as big as this giant caught by John!

So although John has caught some really big sea fish, including a species, of giant flatfish called a halibut which grows to the size of a small car, he started out catching smaller species learning the basic skills, such as casting and finding good fishing spots. The Essex captain has the following advice to someone looking to start sea fishing:

"Do your homework - find out as much as you can before you go and try to get the right bait, tackle, rigs and general information about the venue and species you will be after. Plus, take clothing to suit the time of year and weather and get a accurate weather forecast so you know what to expect."

A typical day afloat on John's boat starts with the anglers meeting the skipper at the harbour and embarking for the rich, deep waters out to sea. There are lots of safety precautions taken and most charter boats, the name for boats you can hire to go fishing from, supply suitable tackle for you to borrow. Just remember to bring warm clothes and lots of drinks and food!

John's first-ever fish was a type of flatfish called a flounder – somewhat smaller this giant halibut, a member of the same family.

Once anchored, the teams got busy tackling up and baiting their rigs.

Once the boat is anchored over an area the skipper thinks holds fish, often a sandbar, gulley, deeper area or channel, sometimes even a wreck, he will give the signal that it's safe to put a line out. A typical basic sea fishing rig consists of a large weight, up to 10oz, at the bottom of the line and two or three hooks on monofilament line booms up the line. The hooks, which seem large by comparison to freshwater hooks (sea fish have much bigger mouths), are baited with big worms called lugworm or ragworm, strips of squid or mackerel or even just shiny lures to tempt mackerel and pollock, which think the flashes are tiny fish.

A rig for bigger fish such as rays and cod is even simpler, with the lead running on the main line on a special slider, a swivel, a few feet of strong mono and a single, large baited hook. A whole squid or mackerel fillet is a great all-round bait for lots of larger species. This is what the lads used to great effect on The Big Fish Off and it'll work in most areas around the UK.

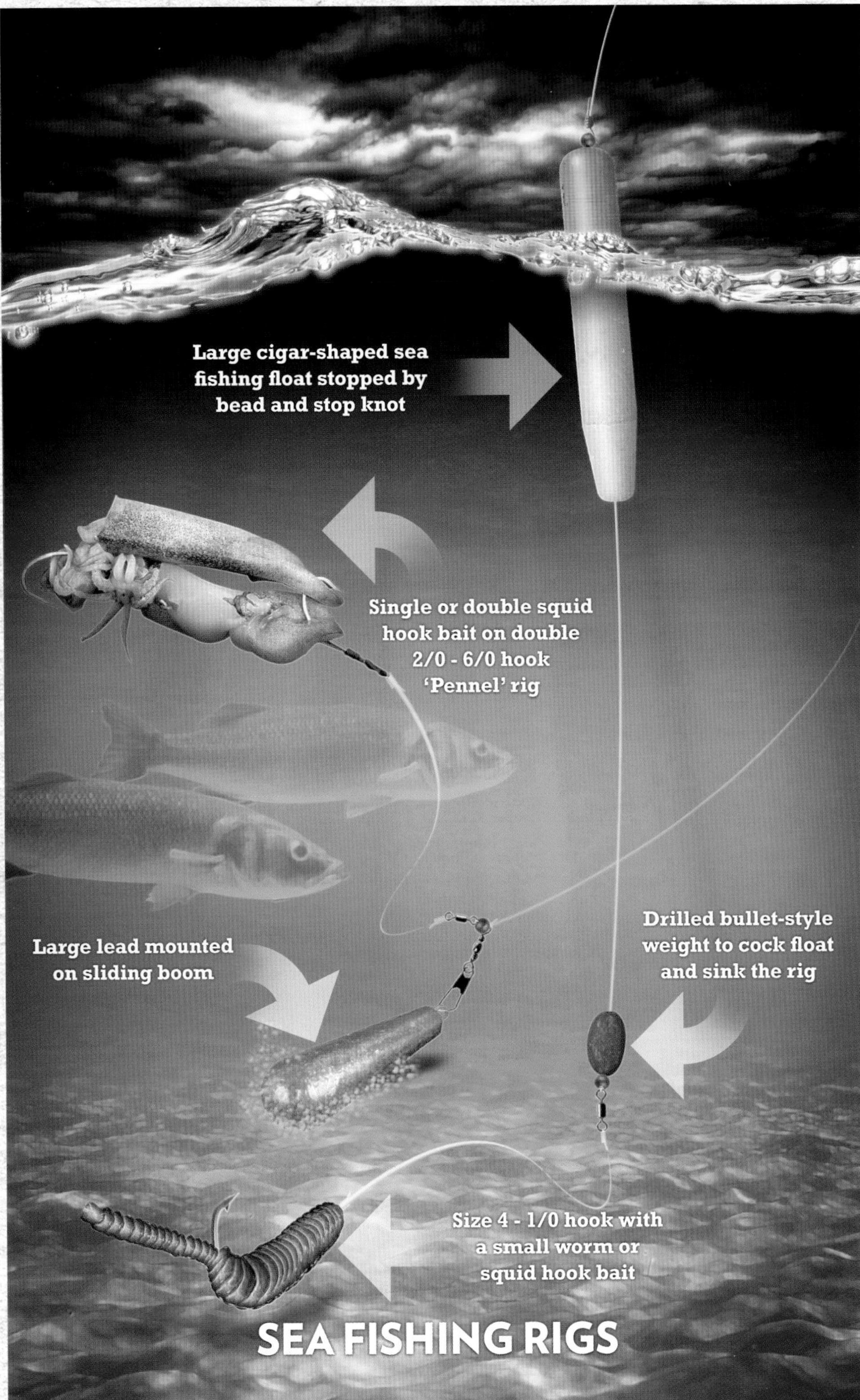

Large cigar-shaped sea fishing float stopped by bead and stop knot
Single or double squid hook bait on double 2/0 - 6/0 hook 'Pennel' rig
Large lead mounted on sliding boom
Drilled bullet-style weight to cock float and sink the rig
Size 4 - 1/0 hook with a small worm or squid hook bait
SEA FISHING RIGS

Under the watchful eye of Skipper John Rawle, Dean shows Steve how to mount a squid bait on the hook.

With the hooks baited, drop the rig over the side of the boat and disengage the bail arm of the reel or the freespool mechanism on a multiplier and let the rig down to the bottom. It's very important to keep some pressure on the spool so the line doesn't peel off too fast – if the line is coming off faster than the lead is pulling it, you'll end up with a big tangle!

You should feel when the lead hits the bottom by a 'thud' sensation that's transmitted up the rod. As soon as this happens, engage the bail arm or freespool and tighten the main line so you're in direct contact with the lead with the rod at a 90-degree angle from your body, over the side of the boat. Try moving it up off the bottom every couple of minutes to attract a bite. When you feel or see a tapping sensation on the rod, this is a fish nibbling the bait, but don't strike immediately or you will probably miss the bite. Wait for a few seconds and a really positive indication before striking and steadily reeling the fish to the surface.

With this sort of fishing, you really don't know what species you might catch but common ones are cod, pollock, wrasse, rays, pouting, dogfish and eels. Changing baits or using larger offerings will attract different species – ask the skipper for advice.

SHOPPING LIST

- Boat fishing rod
- Basic multiplier reel (or a fixed spool reel designed for sea fishing)
- Strong 15-20lb monofilament main line
- Strong swivels
- Sliders (to mount the lead on so it slides up and down the line easily)
- Big leads 4-10oz, both plain and gripper-style (with metal spikes to grip the bottom)
- Heavy mono 30-50lb for the trace
- Scissors
- Big, strong hooks in sizes 1/0 - 6/0
- Ready tied rigs are commonly used in sea fishing and are great for a beginner
- Sharp knife (and case) for cutting bait and filleting fish
- A rig wallet to hold your rigs and traces.

The best sea fishing baits are big and smelly, like this squid!

If the tide is really strong and your lead isn't holding bottom, try letting some line out to form a bow in the main line, this will help the lead grip the bottom. Changing to a heavier lead will also be necessary in most heavily tidal areas. Although plain leads are good for when the tide or current isn't too strong, a lot of sea angling involves the use of gripper leads. These have special metal prongs that dig into the bottom and grip far more efficiently than a plain lead, meaning you can use a smaller lead, which is easier to cast and reel in.

Piers, jetties and breakwaters can be great spots to fish from, but make sure angling is allowed and you have permission. Staying safe is always a priority!

It's a good idea to do a trip or two on a boat, maybe on a seaside holiday as they often have lots of boats offering shorter trips so you can get a taster for sea fishing, before you take the step into other forms of sea angling. This way, you'll have learnt the basics from an experienced skipper like John Rawle, and you'll be more likely to succeed.

Piers, breakwaters and jetties are a good place to broaden your sea angling horizons, but you'll need to make sure you have the right equipment. Carp rods, more usually used in freshwater, can be useful for this sort of fishing as they'll cast quite a heavy lead and bait a fair distance if needed, deal with some larger fish and you won't need to buy a whole new setup. Dean, Ali and the guests used carp rods in their boat fishing challenge and they worked fine, but a specialist sea fishing rod is a wise investment if you're serious about this branch of the sport.

Sea fishing tackle can be bewildering due to the huge variety of species and methods used, but a basic 12ft beachcaster and heavy duty fixed spool reel, similar to the type used for carp angling, loaded with 15lb monofilament line will be usable on all sorts of piers and shore fishing situations. For boat fishing, a shorter rod is ideal as you're often reeling in fish from directly below you and using much heavier leads. The shorter lever the short boat rods offer makes life a lot easier, particularly for the younger angler. If in doubt, most skippers will be only too pleased to point you in the right direction.

Once you have some suitable tackle, John Rawle offers the following advice: "Find out what fishing venues and species you have close to you and ask in tackle shops or local clubs what would be your best option for a novice to catch something."

DID YOU KNOW?

Although the biggest sea species you're likely to encounter in UK waters is likely to be a good bass, cod or ray, our seas were once home to much bigger specimens. The largest, and owner of this impressive tooth, was the megalodon – a 60ft prehistoric shark that lived 2.6-million years ago. A present-day great white shark would have been a mere snack for this giant predator and it would have dwarfed the boat the lads fished from!

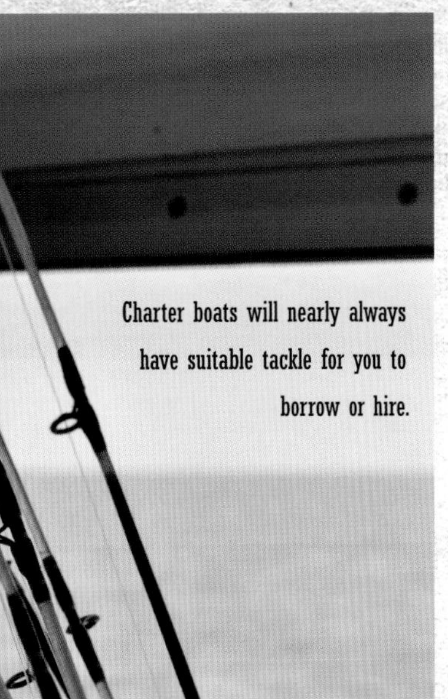

Charter boats will nearly always have suitable tackle for you to borrow or hire.

As before, local clubs and tackle shops are great for taking the next step into sea angling and you'll be able to find your local example online, or by asking fellow anglers. They'll often have teach-ins where you can learn new skills and organised trips or competitions where you can meet fellow anglers and get advice, in fact one of the best ways to learn is to watch an experienced angler and ask questions politely.

Hopefully your research will yield likely venues local to you, assuming you leave near the coast, and you can then work out tide times and how to access the venue. Tides are vital in sea angling as they bring in food for the fish you're targeting, and the fish will follow this trail of food close to shore, where you're fishing. Tide times vary throughout the country but booklets with local times will be available in sea angling tackle shops and marine stores.

Fish on for Team Deano and Steve Collins! One of the great things about sea fishing is that you never really know what's taken your bait.

High tide is key, and it's often the two or three hours either side of high tide that produce bites, with the extra water bringing in fish and their food sources close to shore. A pier is a good place to fish from as it allows you to reach deep water without casting whatever the state of tide but still pay attention to the times, as fish will become more active at these key times.

Safety is a major consideration when sea fishing and

A thornback ray for Ali and Razor, who used a simple rig with squid hook bait.

under no circumstances should you take any risk – no fish is worth losing your life for. Wear a lifejacket on a boat, fish from approved areas on piers and breakwaters and be ultra careful fishing from the shore where the tide can rise quickly.

"Never turn your back on the sea," is an old but very relevant saying – safety has to come first!

Simple rigs and bait are all that's needed to catch many sea species and ready-tied rigs are a good thing to use when you're starting out. Tackle shops will have a good supply and will be able to recommend a suitable rig for the fishing local to them. Generally, a rig called a two-hook (sometimes three) flapper is a good choice as it allows you to use two or three hooks on short traces up a short length of heavy line (for protection against rocks and for extra strength) with a heavy weight on the bottom. This can be cast or lowered into the water, offering two or three different baits, and will catch a wide variety of species.

John prepares part of the catch to be weighed and valued - it's a tense moment for the two teams!

A really fun way of sea fishing is to use a float – just as you would in freshwater but on a slightly larger scale. Again, it's best to find a local pier, jetty or breakwater to try this but you can use a heavy coarse fishing rod and reel without any problems as the fish and weights you're casting are smaller.

The large, cigar-shaped floats and drilled weights are sold in almost all sea fishing tackle shops, often in a kit form to tie

Sea fishing often requires special leads to grip the bottom in fast tides.

the whole rig, with a small hook, hook length, swivel and bead to stop the float when casting, and another bead and stop knot or line stop to stop the float at the desired depth. Make sure the float sits up correctly and try different depths and areas to see what's feeding and where. When the float goes under or starts sailing across the surface, strike – you've got a fish on!

Using a small strip of mackerel, squid or worm section on the hook two or three feet below the surface in the clear water found in many areas of the coast around the UK during the summer months will tempt the eel-like garfish with their pointy snouts, turbo-charged mackerel, hard-fighting pollock and many other colourful species.

Remember to handle your catch with wet hands, unhook gently and carefully return to the water if you're not taking it home to eat!

Skipper John looks on as another spiny thornback ray falls to Ali and Razor's rod.

There are many other possibilities for sea fishing around the UK, and it's a great branch of the sport to explore because there's a fish for every season and being by the sea is never boring! We just hope you don't see anything as horrific as Razor Ruddock and Ali's costume change after their boat trip!

Sea fishing might be challenging, but using the experience you've gained through catching lots of freshwater species will be invaluable as you work your way around the various methods and different tactics.

Always be wary of local size limits for the different species, your own safety and only keep what you need to eat – that way we can make sure there's plenty left for the next generation of Big Fish Off stars!

The possibility of being rescued by these two is reason enough to stay safe by the sea when you're fishing!

MONSTERS!

The British boat-caught record for cod is an amazing 58lb 6oz but the world record stands at well over 100lb, with a 103lb Norwegian monster caught by a German angler the current best. The angler took more than 30 minutes to reel in the huge fish!

Imagine the amount of chips he needed to go with those giant cod steaks!

Typically, big cod require huge baits and heavy tackle, with lures the size of some of the smaller fish the teams caught, to tempt the big-mouthed monsters from the seas around Norway and Iceland. Giant cod thrive in colder water and will eat almost anything - their huge mouths can engulf prey fish and it's quite common for smaller hooked fish to be grabbed by a hungry cod whilst attached to an angler's rod and line! After years of commercial over-fishing, cod stocks are now making a comeback.

Another species the teams encountered on The Big Fish Off, the thornback ray, has a bigger brother that you might not want to encounter on a small boat – the common skate. Weighing more than 200lb and with a with a wingspan of more than 2m fully grown, this giant of the ray family lives in deep water around Scotland and the Celtic Sea. The skate's favourite foods include oysters, shellfish and dead fish and the best bait is a massive chunk of bloody fish on a huge hook, strong monofilament trace and heavy main line with a special harness to help the angler reel the fish in. Fights can last for hours so be prepared!

The world record cod from Norway!

This is a huge common skate, a close relative of the thornback ray.

Michael E...ele
Fishing Book

THE BIG FISH OFF GUIDE TO FISHING

CHAPTER 13 EXOTIC ADVENTURE

Catching large and exotic freshwater fish usually involves travelling all over the world. However, most of us don't have the time, or the inclination, to travel to remote and sometimes dangerous areas in pursuit of a fish... but Gillham's Resort in Thailand offers all of that in one lake where you can fish in comfort for an amazing variety of species. It was the ideal destination for an overseas adventure for The Big Fish Off but anyone can book a holiday to this Asian angling hot spot!

Gillham's is surrounded by some stunning Thai scenery.

Renowned UK angler Stuart Gillham found the perfect location to build his dream water back in 2005, set in stunning surroundings with a freshwater stream nearby, and he then set about digging a lake that would be the perfect environment to grow fish to huge sizes, as well as being somewhere anglers would want to fish.

He then started to stock it with a wide variety of species, some of which were local but others aren't even from the same continent, let alone country, and come from as far afield as South America.

GILLHAMS FACT FILE

The resort is located just a 30 minute or so drive from Krabi Airport, with connecting flights from Bangkok. As well as the fishing, it offers accommodation in luxury lakeside bungalows, but you can also book to just fish for the day if you're travelling through the area, or staying nearby. Its location near to the coast means that many visit Gillhams as part of a family holiday, and there is plenty for non-anglers to do locally – it is practical to fish for a few hours in the morning and then again in the evening, whilst spending the day with the family, as many do. A short taxi ride will get you to some stunning beaches, which also offer some great snorkeling and diving, plus you can go elephant trekking, or take in some of the local culture with a visit to Tiger Cave Temple. Gillhams itself has a restaurant and bar onsite, and serves some fantastic local cuisine, or can cater to those who prefer to stick to English food. It overlooks the lake, and is where everyone winds down when fishing finishes at the end of the day, and compares notes on what they have had, and how they caught it.

Fishing from outside your luxury bungalow is just one of the attractions of fishing at Gillham's.

A decade or so down the line the lake looks better than ever – having been extended to house the 49 different species that now live in it – and a lot of money has been spent to ensure it is somewhere that any angler would want to fish.

Luxury bungalows line one side of the lake, plus a restaurant overlooks it, so you can literally walk out of your door in the morning and start fishing – assuming that you haven't been kept awake by monster fish crashing around all night!

Since opening in 2007, Gillhams has been visited by thousands of anglers from all over the world, some of them experts but also plenty of beginners, or even those who've never fished before but fancied giving it a try whilst on holiday! Two anglers who are big fans of the venue and have visited it numerous times are Ali Hamidi and Dean Macey, and both returned to shoot the finale of The Big Fish Off season two.

They were joined by champion boxer Mitchell Smith and TOWIE reality star Ricky Rayment, who both go fishing but had never experienced anything like Gillhams before!

The well-appointed swims at Gillham's provide a solid platform to battle one of their many monster species from!

This episode pitched TOWIE's Ricky Rayment against pro boxer, Mitchell Smith.

One of the big advantages with coming to this resort is that you don't need to spend a fortune on tackle that you would rarely, if ever, use anywhere else, as everything is provided as part of the package – although it is a good idea to take your own terminal tackle so you can try different set-ups. Plus there are professional guides on hand to help you, who have an intimate knowledge of the venue and the best ways of catching the various species. If you listen to their advice it shouldn't be long before you're attached to a fish that is trying to head towards Bangkok at a rate of knots, and wants to pull your arms off or drag you into the lake!

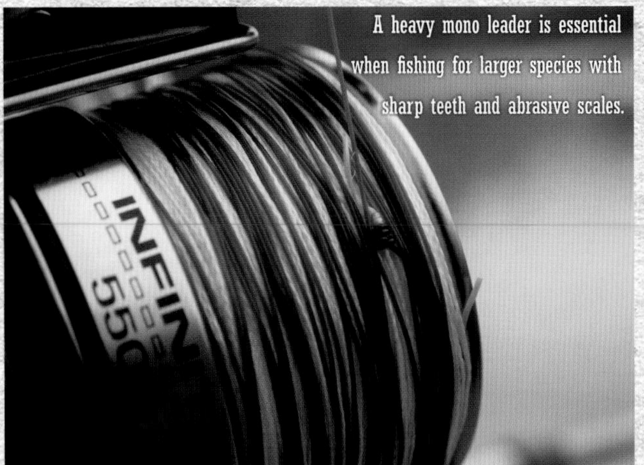

A heavy mono leader is essential when fishing for larger species with sharp teeth and abrasive scales.

You could easily just turn up with your sun tan lotion and still catch fish, but you'll catch a lot more with a bit of preparation.

Taking your own terminal tackle will mean that you're fishing with gear that you're confident in and have much more freedom to experiment with rigs.

Only barbless hooks are allowed, and something strong is essential, with a size 1 Wide Gape B the perfect choice. A strong hook link is also essential, plus some of the fish have abrasive pads in their mouth, so go for either 65lb DuraKord or 85lb ArmaKord XT. Taking a variety of pop-ups in different sizes and colours, plus some artificial corn, is also a good idea, either for fishing popped up, or for critically balancing bottom baits – given that some of the species are naturally filter feeders. Boosting your bait so that the fish home in on it quicker can make a big difference, and the various different flavours of Goo are ideal as they give off a cloud of colour and flavour – mixing them with locally bought coconut milk can also be deadly for the Mekong cats.

It is well worth taking plenty of PVA with you as well – Funnelweb mesh is perfect if you want the bag to break down very quickly in the warm water, but also take some Solidz bags to get everything down to the bottom before it begins to melt.

SHOPPING LIST

The main tackle items you need to fish at Gillham's (and similar destinations) are all supplied, but it's a good idea to bring a few essentials. Remember, you'll be flying out there, so you'll have to think carefully about what you can fit into the hold. Here's what we'd take for an exotic adventure...

- **Your favourite pop-ups**
- **Bottles of Goo in various flavours**
- **85lb ArmaKorda XT**
- **65lb DuraKorda**
- **Size 1 Wide Gape B hooks**
- **Funnelweb PVA mesh**
- **Polarised sunglasses**
- **Mosquito repellant**
- **Sun tan lotion**

The main tackle items you need to fish at Gillham's (and similar destinations) are all supplied, but it's a good idea to bring a few essentials.

A selection of Goos will add attraction to loose-feed pellets, drawing the big 'uns into your swim in no time!

Strong, simple rigs with high-attract hook baits and a small PVA bag of pellets are all that's needed to target many of the species at Gillham's.

BEHIND THE SCENES

During the filming of The Big Fish Off 2 finale, Ali Hamidi and his partner Ricky Rayment found that regular recasting and highly attractive baits was the key to their success. Clipping up was essential to ensure they were recasting to the same spot each time, and a large Funnelweb PVA bag of pellets soaked in a combination of different flavoured Goo was added. The PVA bag was doubled up to ensure that it stayed on until it reached the lakebed - with the Goo leaving a trail down through the water - as the warm water speeds up the PVA's melt rate. For a fish with such a large mouth, small hookbaits work really well, especially buoyant ones such as the snowman rigs which Ali and Ricky opted for to land the only Mekong of the challenge.

WHAT CAN YOU CATCH?

With so many different species in the lake you never quite know what is going to be on the other end when your bite alarm sounds or the float goes under – it could even be an IGFA World Record, as the fishery currently holds three of those! Six of the species in the lake go to over 100lb, and some of them are an awful lot bigger than that!

If you're using a dead fish as bait then you could easily find yourself connected to a huge 8ft long arapaima, which go to over 500lb in this venue and are regularly seen rolling on the surface. Or it might be one of the giant freshwater stingray which run to over 200lb and can have a 'wingspan' of 6ft! The native predatory Chao Praya catfish, which are often seen swimming

The lads were ecstatic to win the Mekong Challenge with this monster!

near the surface, grow to 130lb, plus wallagoo leeri (another type of catfish) top out at 110lb, and the much sought-after and beautifully marked Amazon redtail catfish, will all take deadbaits.

Gillham's is home to nearly 50 species, with the Amazon red tail catfish one of the more colourful.

Mitchell Smith wrestles a Siamese carp that's a heavyweigtht in the fish world!

Fishing with boilies or pellets will give you a good chance of hooking Thailand's largest indigenous freshwater species, the Mekong catfish. These filter-feeders are almost impossible to locate and catch in the wild, but in lakes like Gillhams they are happy to eat anglers' bait and are renowned for their fighting prowess – sometimes taking several hours to land should you hook one of the 200lb-plus beasts. These tactics will also account for another of Thailand's home-grown monsters, the Siamese carp, which again are almost impossible to catch in rivers, but in this lake there are plenty to target, with 50 of them topping 100lb and the chance of one over 200lb!

Whilst many anglers visit the complex to target these big fish, there are also smaller species to go for, which are great fun on lighter tackle, and some of them have stunning markings and colours.

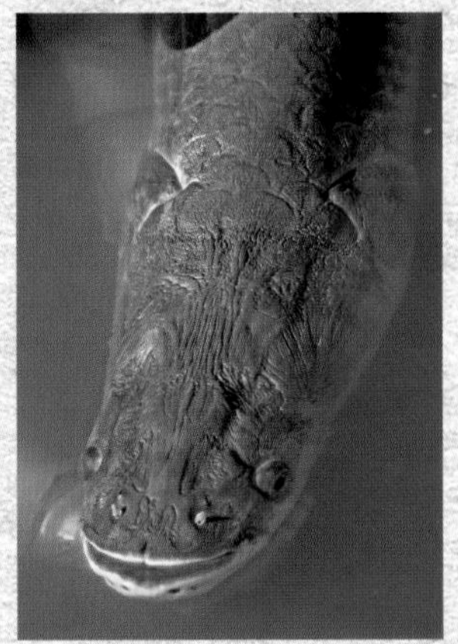

The huge head of an arapaima - one of the biggest freshwater fish in the world. They grow to over 500lb at Gillham's!

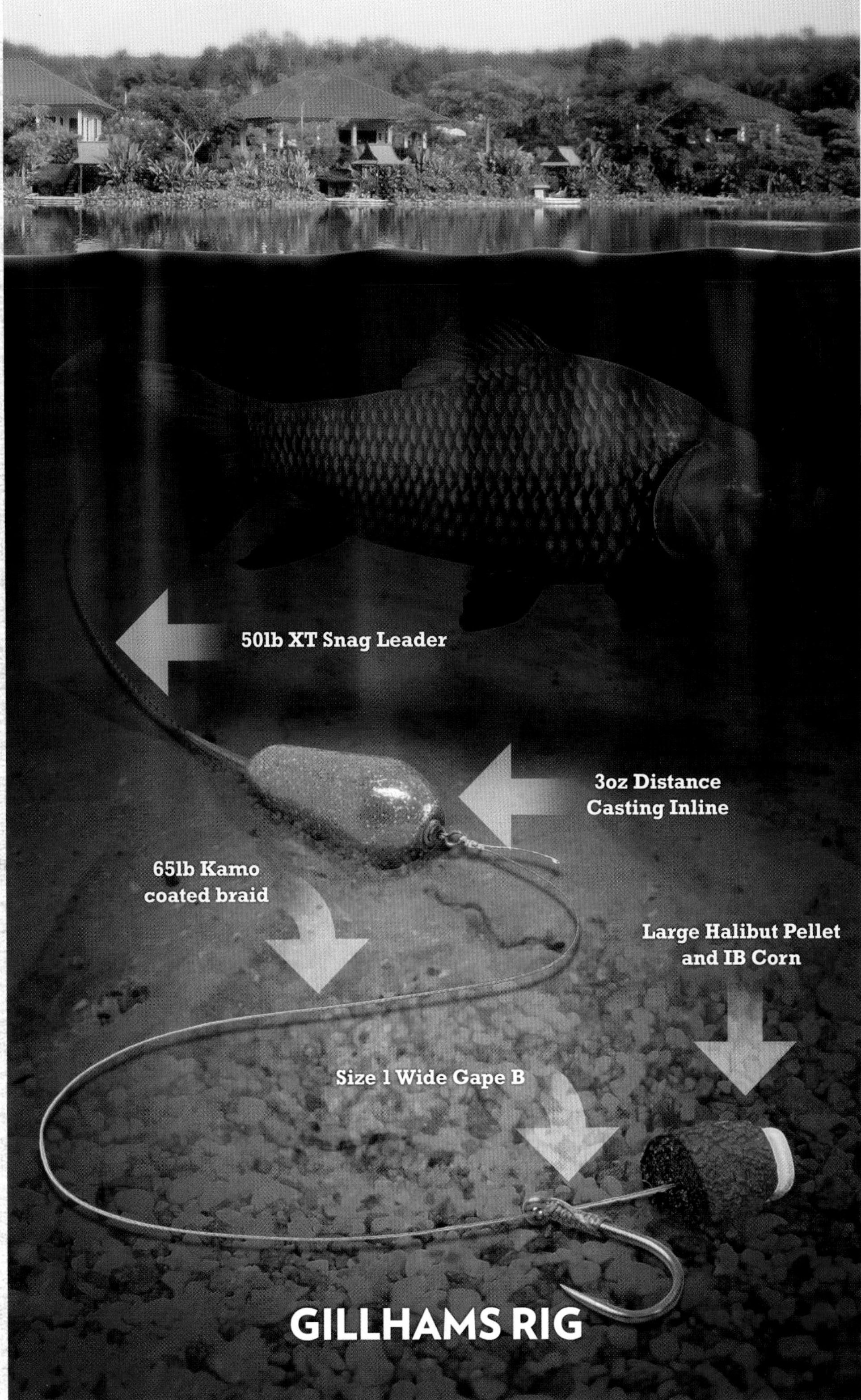
50lb XT Snag Leader
3oz Distance
Casting Inline
65lb Kamo
coated braid
Large Halibut Pellet
and IB Corn
Size 1 Wide Gape B
GILLHAMS RIG

Smaller species as this stunning arawana are great fun on light tackle.

Smaller species as this stunning arawana are great fun on light tackle.

These include arawana, and firewood catfish from South America, plus the giant featherback, giant gourami, Asian redtail and Julian's golden carp, which are found locally.

The lake is well-stocked but not to the extent where it affects the growth rate of the fish – they've had Siamese carp put on up to 30lb in a year! – and it still presents a challenge if you're going to make the best of your stay.

If you fancy trying something a bit different for a few hours, the complex also includes a lake that was originally for lure and fly fishing only, but now allows all methods. It can be great fun using lighter gear and holds a wide variety of species – but you will need all of your own kit if you want to try lures or the fly. As well as the species that will take a lure, if you fish on bait you'll catch various species including Julian's golden carp on float fished corn.

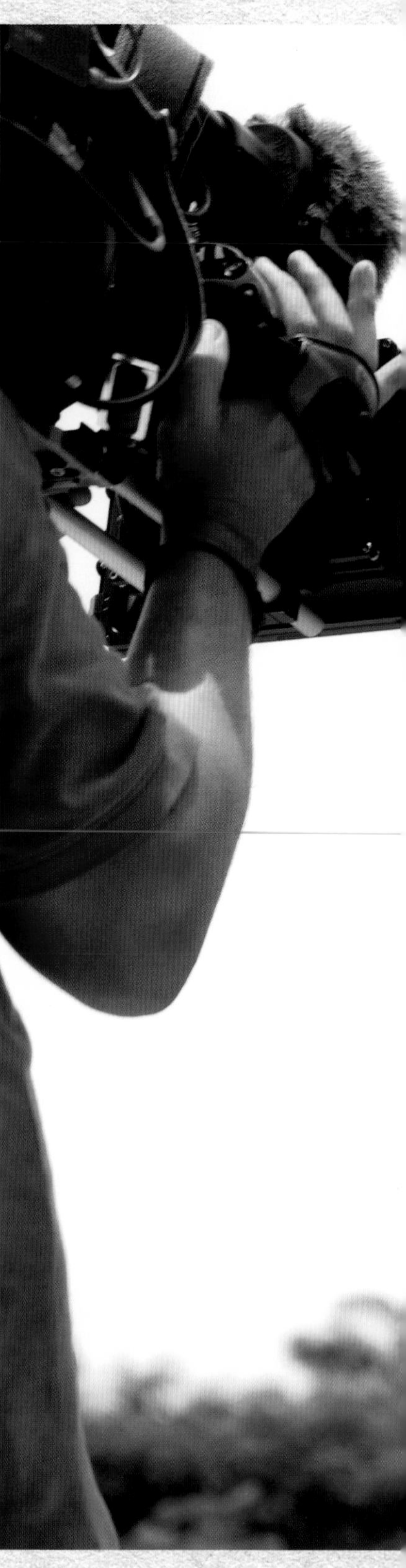

The teams endured some arm-aching battles with giant Mekong catfish and Siamese carp. Even Dean looks tired!

THE BIG FISH OFF GUIDE TO FISHING

MONSTERS!

Many of the anglers visiting Gillhams will never have experienced anything like the fish that they could hook into!

Some, such as arapaima and Mekongs for their sheer size alone, but others for their strange looks, bright colours, or mouths full of razor sharp teeth!

The biggest fish that a lot of anglers from the UK will have any experience with is a carp or pike, or maybe a catfish, and perhaps even a trip to France or Spain in pursuit of larger ones. But the larger species found at Gillhams are on another level when it comes to just how hard they pull back, and the weights they grow to. That also means that the tackle you'll be using is very different to that back at home, with 10ft 6lb, or even 8lb, test curve rods being the norm, along with big pit reels loaded with 40lb mono, or heavy braid.

Some of the species such as the alligator gar and snakeheads have proper teeth, and even many of those that don't, such as the catfish, still have sharp 'pads' in their mouths that will destroy standard carp hook link materials in no time.

Specimens like this huge arapaima require heavy tackle and big hooks - quite different to the equipment you might use in the UK.

A size 1 hook will look big compared to what we tend to use in the UK, but once you see it in the mouth of one of these giants you'll probably be left wondering why you aren't using something bigger!

Acknowledgements

Loads of people deserve our gratitude for help during the filming of The Big Fish Off and the compilation of this book! In no particular order, we'd like to thank:

Richard Stewart

Ben Hervey-Murray

John Hannent

Gary Newman

John Rawle

Kurt Thorpe

Jack Perks

Nik Warner

Adam Baxter

Matt Ford

Ed Noel

Joe Saunders

West Mersea Oyster Bar

Steve Sands at Churchwood Fisheries

Churchgate Fisheries

Will Barnard at Thames Water's Walthamstow Reservoirs

Peter Rolfe (for help with the crucian chapter!)

Colchester Postal & Telecom Angling Club

Lake John Fishery

David De Vere at Bury Hill Fisheries

Henham Fishery

Colchester Angling Preservation Society

Gillham's Resort

Basildon Sporting Village

Basildon Borough Council